PENGUIN BOOKS

REFLECTIONS

Idries Shah was born in 1924 into a family that traces itself through the Prophet Mohammed and to the Sassanian Emperors of Persia and, beyond that, back to the year 122 B.C.—perhaps the oldest recorded lineage on earth. Shah is the author of sixteen books published in five languages and forty-five editions throughout the world. Their subject matter ranges over travel, bibliography, literature, humor, philosophy, and history, but their author is most prominent for his writings on Sufi thought as it applies to the cultures of both East and West. Despite the extraordinary success of these books, Shah refuses newspaper interviews and declines to play the role of a "guru," preferring hard and silent work in his chosen milieu of thinkers and artists. He has recently been awarded the Dictionary of International Biography's Certificate of Merit for Distinguished Service to Human Thought. In addition to *Reflections*, Penguin Books publishes Shah's *Thinkers of the East* and *Caravan of Dreams*.

IDRIES SHAH

REFLECTIONS

Penguin Books Inc
New York · Baltimore

Penguin Books Inc
72 Fifth Avenue
New York, New York 10011

Penguin Books Inc
7110 Ambassador Road
Baltimore, Maryland 21207

First published by The Octagon Press, England, 1968
Published in Penguin Books 1972
Reprinted 1974

Copyright © Idries Shah, 1968

Printed in the United States of America by
Kingsport Press, Inc., Kingsport, Tennessee

Library of Congress Catalog Card Number 75–171352

CONTENTS

FOREWORD

Once upon a time, not so very long ago, a certain building was infested by mice. The people in charge decided to kill them.

One night they put down mouse-killing poison. But the next morning the poison had been eaten.

'We shall change the type of poison,' the people said, and they made another attempt. But this second lethal dose the mice also ate happily, and left signs that they were thriving on their new diet.

It was decided to use old-fashioned, spring-operated mousetraps. These were baited with succulent cheese to tempt the poison-proof mice.

But the mice refused to touch the cheese.

One of the mouse-catchers now had an inspiration. He thickly coated the cheese in the traps with poison. 'Perhaps the mice have developed a liking for poison: it may even be doing them good,' he reasoned.

The new plan was put into operation late one evening. The following morning the spring-traps were full of strong and healthy mice.

From this story could be extracted all kinds of morals and teachings. But it is quoted here because it is absolutely true.*

Do you imagine that fables exist only to

* London *Daily Mail*, December 2, 1967, p. 9. col. 3.

amuse or to instruct, and are based upon fiction? The best ones are delineations of what happens in real life, in the community and in the individual's mental processes.

IDRIES SHAH

THE AMBITIOUS RATS

Once upon a time there were some rats.

Nothing remarkable happened to them until they started to develop ambition.

Their ambition took the form of wanting to be much, much bigger than they were at the time.

Almost all their activities began to be directed towards this end.

In the course of time they started to breed as larger and larger rats.

The first noteworthy event in their history was when men, realising that these rats were large enough, began to hunt them for their skins.

The second event was when other men realised that they could trap them and exhibit them as the 'biggest rats in the world'.

The third important event will, no doubt, be reported to you when it takes place.

DRAMATIC

A well developed sense of the dramatic has values beyond what people usually imagine. One of these is to realise the limitations of a sense of the dramatic.

THE HIGHEST PRINCIPLES

There was once a selfish and arrogant man. He had early learned, however, that he could conceal and yet indulge his harmful proclivities by calling them something else. He affected to preach and to practise perfection, and quite easily fell into a self-deceptive cast of mind.

He found fault with others in the belief that he was trying to improve human behaviour in general and specific instances in particular. People became terrified of his criticisms: based as they manifestly were upon the highest principles of their own culture.

None could fault his high morality. The society to which he belonged had no provision for cases when moralism became a disease. The only rôle which the community could provide for him was that of a guardian of the public ethic.

His demand for nothing less than the best became such a habit with him that, one day when he became ill he refused to be treated by any doctor who did not possess the highest possible academic and clinical qualifications.

Now, he happened to be suffering from appendicitis: an ailment which can be dealt with by any ordinary practitioner. But, possessed by his own importance, irrevocably linked with his conception of the 'best man for the task', he started to travel from one town to another, seeking greater and greater surgical paragons.

Each time he met a doctor he feared that the man might not be good enough.

Finally, as a successful operation became an immediate necessity to save his life, he found himself in a village where the only person with any knowledge of anatomy was—the local butcher.

He was a truly excellent butcher. But, as a result of his manfully energetic, irreproachably dedicated, efforts, our friend the reputedly virtuous man for whom second-best was no use at all, bled to death.

POINT OF VIEW

Saadi of Shiraz, in his *Bostan,* stated an important truth when he told this miniature tale:

A man met another, who was handsome, intelligent and elegant. He asked him who he was. The other said: 'I am the Devil.'

'But you cannot be,' said the first man, 'for the devil is evil and ugly.'

'My friend,' said Satan, 'you have been listening to my detractors.'

DIFFERENT EVERY TIME

A Sufi master was visited by a perplexed Seeker-after-Truth, who said to him:

'I have only one question to ask. Why is it that, wherever I go, I always seemed to get different pieces of advice from Sufis?'

The master answered:

'Come with me for a walk through this town, and we shall see what we can discover about this mystery.'

They went into the market-place, and the Sufi asked a greengrocer:

'Tell me, what time of prayer is it?'

The greengrocer said:

'The time for the morning prayer.'

They continued their walk. After some time the Sufi asked a tailor:

'What prayer-time is it?'

The tailor answered:

'It is the time of the midday prayer.'

After spending more time in conversation and companionship with the Seeker, the Sufi approached another man, this time a bookbinder. He asked him:

'What time of prayer is it?'

The man replied:

'It is now the time of the afternoon prayer.'

The Sufi turned to his companion and said:

'Do you want to continue the experiment, or are you now satisfied that virtually the same question can elicit almost totally dif-

6

ferent answers, all of them corresponding to
the current truth?'

HISTORY

History is not usually what has happened.
History is what some people have thought
to be significant.

AFFECTION AND REGARD

It is possible to have great affection and
regard for individuals and groups of people
without in any way reducing one's awareness
of their currently poor capacity for understanding and preserving their heritage.

The present state of ignorance about distant and former cultures is not unique to this
time. Unfortunately, though, the people of
our time are not employing their superior
resources to retrieve and develop the rem-
nants of wider knowledge possessed else-
where and also at other times.

This is because, while the tools and the
general freedom are there for the first time,
desire, resolution and breadth of vision are
absent, also for the first time.

The endowment is therefore at risk. For
the first time.

7

FORMS OF LOVE

A man once decided that all perfection and beauty was in the tree. It gave fruit, shelter, materials for manufactures. It did this, too, without apparently making demands. It was there for 'good' purposes. So he taught people that 'tree' was 'good'.

Everyone eventually worshipped in forests and groves, and they loved trees. This preoccupation diverted most human attention for perhaps 10,000 years. These people mistook the immediate for the Real. So it is with man's present ideas about love.

His most sublime ideas about love, if he but knew it, can be called the lowest of the possible perceptions of real love.

WHAT I SAY

If you are uninterested in what I say, there's an end to it.

If you like what I say, please try to understand which previous influences have made you like it.

If you like some of the things I say, and dislike others, you could try to understand why.

If you dislike all I say, why not try to find out what formed your attitude?

THE OYSTER

An oyster, lying open on the ocean bed, felt a loose pearl washed over it.

The oyster closed its shell, and the pearl fell into a rock-crevice.

After tremendous effort, the oyster managed to retrieve the pearl and placed it on a leaf just beside it.

'This bribe may prevent the oyster-catchers from taking me,' it thought, for it knew something about men who sought for pearls.

When a pearl-diver, however, was ultimately in the vicinity, his eyes were alert for oyster shells, not pearls lying about loose.

So he took the oyster, which as it happened did not contain a pearl—and the real pearl rolled away. It has not yet been rediscovered.

DROWNING

To drown in treacle is just as unpleasant as to drown in mud.

People today are in danger of drowning in information; but, because they have been taught that information is useful, they are more willing to drown than they need be.

If they could handle information, they would not have to drown at all.

THE LIGHTNING AND THE OAK TREE

The lightning said to the oak tree:
'Stand aside, or take what is coming to you!'

CAUSES

As important a fact as any individual cause on earth is the virtual incapacity of the human individual to distinguish between a genuine cause and one which is foisted upon him by pressure, environment, propaganda, conditioning.

If people had the sense they pretend to have, they would seek the means to make this fundamental distinction perceptible.

Hardly anyone makes this effort. This is partly because it is an invisible but powerful part of their culture to teach that conditioned emotionality and 'causes' whose necessity, urgency or rightness is only conditioned into them are, necessarily, right.

TRUST

None should say: 'I can trust,' or ' I cannot trust' until he is master of the option, of trusting or not trusting.

INDIRECT ROUTE

A man worked for many years, seeking ways to become famous.

Eventually, when he had amassed a great deal of money and was able to afford the services of a public relations specialist, he realised what he could have aimed for from the first.

CHANGING SENSE OF HUMOUR

It is encouraging that statements thought improbable enough to be quoted as humorous literary mistakes can, in under ten years, be regarded as serious and even perceptive.

This is an example of such a 'howler':

'Faith is that quality by which we believe what we should otherwise think was false.'*

THE OLDER THE BETTER

The intrusion of the doctrine of 'the older the better' is a characteristic of the irrationality which must break out somewhere in people who are trying too hard to be rational.

* (Cecil Hunt), *The Best Howlers,* London, 1949. p. 36.

SIGNWRITERS

Why are signwriters anonymous? In order to understand this, we have to go back into history.

At one time, you see, signwriters were not anonymous.

People used to respect and to applaud them, and also employed their signs and posters for information and directions.

But, after a time, the rôles of the people, the signs and the signwriters got out of balance.

'Why did you make that arrow so big?' people started to ask; and 'This sign only expresses the personality of the artist—I'll not follow its content.'

And so on.

Now, because people had become more interested in people than in things, without being able to deepen their knowledge of people, a decision had to be taken: whether the signs or the writers were more necessary or important.

That is why signwriters are mostly anonymous . . .

Now they are getting better known again.

HEAT AND COLD

One day, heat and cold came to the conclusion that they were too far apart:

'Co-existence is the answer,' they resolved.

Both of them thought that the new arrangement was fine, and they huddled together, mutually comforting, until each heard some-one say:

'Isn't it strange that nothing is hot nor cold these days? The only temperature that seems to exist is warmth.'

So they separated, and the only warmth to be found after that was in things not yet hot, or on the way to becoming cold.

INSPIRATIONS

People who speak or act in an ordinary fashion are most likely to be those who have been the recipients of higher experiences. But because these do not rage around, wild-eyed, people think that they are very ordinary folk and therefore not aware of anything unknown to the general run of man.

LOCAL AND REAL TRUTH

The existence of relative truth does not prove the non-existence of universal truth.

A HARE

There once was a hare who was proud that he had such fine, long ears.

He realised, however, that the tips became icy on very cold days.

So he decided to keep his eyes open all the time so that he would see the cold coming in time to avoid it.

ATTENTION

People demand attention. The right kind of attention at suitable times leads to the maintenance of a thriving individual. Ignorance of attention-need leads to too much or too little intake of attention.

Ignorance of the attention-factor, too, leads to mistaking attention-demand for something else. This something else is the social, psychological or other ritual which people think is the essential reason for human contact. In fact it is only one ingredient of human contact and interchange.

It is a basic error to imagine that only a human being can be involved in the attention-situation. Some of the most important attention-situations concern real or imagined sources of attention other than human ones.

FREEDOM

'I always looked at the alternatives,' said
the sheep: 'I can munch or I can bite.'

GENERALISATIONS
ARE PERILOUS

It is often stated that generalisations are
dangerous. This is true: but only when it *is*
true. Generalisations are useful, even essential, in certain situations, dangerous in others. To say: 'Motor-cars are dangerous' is
useful for a child, for a period of its life.
After that it may become a barrier to crossing the road. At that point other generalisations are supplied, to protect the child for a
period or to carry it a stage further towards
learning.

A huge area of human life and thought
requires the intelligent use of generalisations: which includes using them, modifying
them and superseding them.

ARMS AND LEGS

Many people who cannot reach higher think
that their arms should be longer. In some
cases you can see that it is their legs which
are too short.

FUNCTION

'To think I never realised what a good doorstop I'd make,' said the heavy book to itself, settling down.

ADULT TODDLERS

Many problems arise in current cultures because numerous adults behave like infants, while it is part of the convention to treat such behaviour as that of—adults. But parents would not allow it in their own children.

These people are still educable, even though their education might have to be similar to that given to children. We make few facile assumptions about 'natural' or 'basic' knowledge being already in children. Oddly, we assume that adults know a lot of things which they do not.

PRESENCE AND ABSENCE

A certain person may have, as you say, a wonderful presence: I do not know. What I do know is that he has a perfectly delightful absence.

CARPENTER'S SHOP

I went into a carpenter's shop.

'Why is your door broken?' I said.

'People come to a carpenter to have their own work done, not to ask about his,' he said.

Sometime later I saw another carpenter in his workshop.

'Why has your table only three legs?' I asked.

'I hadn't noticed that,' he said.

And there was, on another occasion, another woodworker.

'Your window-frame is splintered, and has been so for some time,' I told him.

'I am too busy to mend it,' he answered, 'I have been making chairs for sale.'

COMPREHENSION

Man does not have a capacity of instant comprehension.

So rare is the knowledge of how to train this, that most people, and almost all institutions, have compromised by playing upon man's proneness to conditioning and indoctrination instead.

The end of that road is the ant-heap; or, at best, the beehive.

THE NAIL

A man and a nail had a conversation.
The nail said:
'I have often wondered, during my years sticking here in this panel, what my fate is to be.'
The man said:
'Latent in your situation may be a tearing out with pincers, a burning of wood and a fall, the rotting of the plank—so many things.'
Said the nail:
'I should have known better than to ask such foolish questions! Nobody can foresee even one thing that might happen in the future, let alone a variety of them, and all so very different and unlikely.'
And he waited, having learned this nail-wisdom, until someone else should come along, someone who would talk intelligently, and not threaten him.

STUDY

The practice of study only too often makes people mere repeaters and producers of clichés and sayings. Such study has been all but wasted. But the product has taken the form in which we find it because it is an unsuitable graft upon an unprepared basis.

ORIGINAL PERFECTION

He was yellow, plump and soft, his surface broken up, the movements ungainly, full of uncertainty, covetousness and hunger.

His main desire was to attain a state in which he would want nothing, need to make no movement, present a smooth, uniform and delicately satisfying face to the world.

He did not realise that he was a chicken who wanted to be an egg.

HUMILITY

Humility cannot be taught by propaganda, though slavery can. Shouting for humility is a form of arrogance. One of my most abiding recollections is of a priest at a religious occasion once roaring, in the most threatening way imaginable:

'O our Lord God, we most *humbly* pray . . . !'

Real humility is not always the same as apparent humility. Remember that fighting against self-conceit is still fighting: and that it will tend to suppress it temporarily. It does not cure anything.

Remember, too, that humility itself does not bring an automatic reward: it is a means to an end. It enables a person to operate in a certain manner.

WASPS

A king who feared wasps once decreed that they were abolished.

As it happened, they did him no harm. But he was eventually stung to death by scorpions.

DIFFERENT AND THE SAME

Supposing for a moment that you were not yourself, but a visitor among men, ignorant of their ways of behaving and their elaborate habits of self-deception.

One of the first things which you would notice is that a large part of people's time is spent in thinking and acting just like other people, while at the same time they energetically claim that they are 'different'.

You would conclude that this predeliction stemmed from a warp of thinking, and was a serious barrier to making use even of the things which they do understand.

It gives rise to one of the major customs of the human tribe: 'Let's pretend, and let's forget that we are pretending, so that we can then conscientiously deny it.'

CHOICE

The word 'choice' is a fraud while people choose only what they have been taught to choose.

OCCASION

A man called Aslam found himself one day following what he took to be a wedding procession. He called out:

'Rejoice for this happy occasion!'

But, since it was a funeral, the mourners took hold of him and objected strenuously.

'What was the right thing to say?' he asked.

'You should have said: "Mercy upon you!"' they replied.

Soon afterwards another procession came along, while Aslam was still memorising his line.

'Mercy upon him!' he cried.

But it was a wedding party, and the guests took him severely to task, saying:

'Learn that you should have been saying: "What an auspicious occasion!"'

They coached him in this phrase until he was word-perfect, and then they let him go.

Another party of people approached him, and he called out:

'What an auspicious occasion!'

They were furious. 'We are lost and do not know the way, and you call that an auspicious occasion!'

So they beat him a little. Then they said:

'Can you tell us the way to such-and-such a place?'

'I'm a stranger here myself,' said Aslam. They rained blows upon him, afterwards explaining: 'We don't use the word "stranger"—it is unlucky.'

'Well, then,' he said, 'I am not a stranger.' At the word 'stranger' they fell to beating him again.

Then the police arrived. They took him to court and had him fined: because, in that town, a person who was not a stranger and who did not direct honest travellers was guilty of a crime.

'This is the place for me,' said Aslam aloud, when he was released, 'because I am learning so many things that I did not know before.'

But someone overheard, and he was arrested again, because, according to the traditions of that country, it was both socially and legally wrong to say: 'This is the place for me.'

As soon as he was let out of the court, Aslam exclaimed:

'This is not the place for me!'

So they took him and imprisoned him for saying things critical of the community, or likely to cause social dissatisfaction.

SUBORDINATES

Almost every day I am reminded of Saadi's reflection that there is no senseless tyranny like that of subordinates.

22

THE LIZARD AND THE SPIDER

A lizard and a spider met. The lizard said: 'What do you eat?' and the spider replied: 'Flies.'

'So do I,' said the lizard, 'it seems that we are suitable companions.'

They set up house together.

One night they were out catching flies. A cat approached. In the instant before it pounced on him, the lizard cried to the spider:

'A cat is going to catch me, what shall I do?'

The spider called back:

'Just spin out some web and make your escape into this tiny hole where I am.'

While the lizard was trying to understand this, the cat caught him.

UNKNOWN

There are, literally, thousands of wise people, unknown to the ordinary man. They teach in a manner which is not recognised as teaching by the herd. They continuously influence man.

People who respond to authority-figures and weird things are unable to make any contact with them. Other people lack information and preparation.

REPORT ON THE
PLANET EARTH

A body of celestial beings, who wanted to develop their influence upon the people of the earth, commissioned an experienced and independent investigator to provide them with a feasibility report.

When he came back, he said:

'Here is a complete analysis of the situation. To get through to mankind, you must promise happiness to those who are sad, and threaten with distress those who are happy. They are all to be exposed to tension, anxiety, joy and repetition. They must be induced to think, when they are hypocrites, that they are honest and straightforward. You will also sanctify self-indulgence, by making people enjoy suffering and then tell them that they are not enjoying it, because it is a punishment.'

'But this is terrible!' exclaimed the celestial ones. 'We could never do that. To turn people into automata, to manipulate them . . .'

'Now listen,' said the expert, 'do you or do you not want to extend your territory? If you plan expansion in this field, you must remember that—for thousand of years—your competitors have been ahead of you. They are well established there, and they are successful. In fact there are only a very few, quite insignificant, exceptions . . .'

THE DEMON AND
THE WISE MAN

A demon was sitting outside the house of a wise man one day, when a Seeker-after-Truth came to the door.

'Aha!' thought the devil, 'I must dust off my temptations.'

So he prepared all kinds of snares and transmitted them into the disciple's mind. He conjured up pictures of fame and prosperity, of dignity and honour, of power and pleasures.

But the devout one, through his many years' study and discipline, had acquired defences against all these things, and he fought them down as soon as ever they entered his head.

Then he went into the presence of the Master. The demon crept invisibly into the room, and watched. The Seeker-after-Truth first noticed that the teacher was seated on the floor, and his heart warmed to him: 'This is indeed a humble man,' he thought.

Then he realised that the Sage was taking no notice of him at all. He began to wonder whether this was, after all, the man for him. Then he saw that the Sage was dressed in clothes different from those which he expected, and his faith in him began to waver. When the Master had spoken a few words, the would-be disciple soon realised that he did not like him at all.

He quit the house, saying: 'My search must still continue.'

When he was disappearing into the distance, the Master, through his inner faculties, spoke to the demon, saying: 'You need not have worried, trickster—he was yours all the time, you know.'

DEBUNKING

Once upon a time people used to become established as authority-figures and were then respected for centuries, even thousands of years.

Then came the age of debunking, which is still with us. People started to debunk almost as soon as a reputation had been built up.

But there is another phase now: people are being debunked almost before they become famous.

IMPROVEMENT

If you want to make an ordinary man happy, or think that he is happy, give him money, power, flattery, gifts, honours.

If you want to make a wise man happy—improve yourself!

THE TWO DEMONS

A junior devil said to a senior one:

'If only we could stop man from using sovereign intellect! Can we not devise a scheme to block his efforts towards self-development?'

The elder answered:

'My child, it has been done already! Man was aeons ago convinced that he possesses choice and sovereign intellect as some sort of gift. He has long since—with only a few insignificant exceptions—ceased to listen to anyone who says that he has a real intellect waiting to be developed.'

CONTRARIES

Try to remember, as a corrective against automatic assumptions, the story of the wise dervish and the mother.

A woman was carrying her baby down a hill when she saw what looked like a reverend dervish, and she asked him to bless her child.

He immediately started to curse it.

This made her weep bitterly, and regard the man as utterly evil.

What she did not know about him was that he belonged to a realm where things always went by contraries.

MOTIVES OF THE RABBIT

A fox was running through a glade, when he saw a rabbit bolting into a burrow.

As the rabbit sat there, quivering, the fox went up to the entrance to the hole. He said:

'Are you afraid?'

'Not afraid in the usual sense,' said the rabbit, 'but I am meditating upon the evils of creatures, and my own shortcomings, my sins and my need to do good . . .'

He went on like this for quite a time, for he had indeed convinced himself by now that some higher power had affected him.

The fox, thoroughly bored, padded off on his way.

And the rabbit? He became the founding father of the rabbit divines, who spent their time alternately frightening themselves individually and each other, collectively.

READING A BOOK

People say that they want to learn, but if they don't know how and don't want to learn how, nobody can do much more than inform them of the facts.

Remember the man who, told to read a book, said: 'No, I tried that once and it didn't work.'

GOAT-LEADER

Some goats at pasture saw a lion in the distance.

A few of them were alarmed, and ran to the leader of the herd for his help and interpretation.

The lion came nearer, looked at the goats and roared.

'No need to worry,' said the goat-leader, 'and I can prove it. See, what an ugly colour his fur is! And, as for his bleat—you can tell by that that he'll never amount to anything.'

BROTH AND COOKS

A man told me how much time and effort he had spent going from one guru to another.

'Too many cooks, I suppose you'll tell me, spoil the broth,' he said.

He thought I was a guru of the kind which is most publicly plentiful. Among this plentitude of gurus, they often take me for one of their number, too.

The consequence of being the reluctant recipient of numerous guru confidences is that I have realised that the reverse of the proverb is only too tragically true.

It may confidently be enunciated that:

'Too many broths spoil the cooks.'

TRAPPED RAT

A rat became trapped in a natural rocky labyrinth one day.

The passages were so winding and confused, and the entrances so few and so small, that this rat, as the time passed, became more and more frenzied, thinner, fierce, and obsessed by the need to attack whatever it was that he imagined had projected him into this fate.

It so happened that at the very moment when he was thin enough to get through an aperture to freedom, a dog was terrorising the whole rat community just outside.

When the trapped rat appeared, he took one look at this dog, and in front of the assembled rats, leapt upon it and sunk his teeth into its jugular vein.

He was, of course, unanimously elected 'greatest rat of all time'.

Now this rat was a hero. Does this mean that real heroes do not exist, that all is accident? No, but it does mean that when rats are trapped they will try and will believe anything.

'I'

Contemplate much less the 'I shall progress,' than the 'I' stand in '*my* way'.

THE RICH MAN
WHO WAS A BEGGAR

Once upon a time, and this is a true story, there was a rich man. He had inherited vast wealth. Putting it all away and retaining just enough for the journey, he travelled to a country where he was not known, to see whether, if he had not been born rich, he would have been able to make his fortune.

After many vicissitudes, this man amassed great riches, and proved to himself that he had indeed the talent to make money. But, in the process, he learnt many other things.

Now he had a great deal of money and wanted to give it away, so that it might be shared with those who had little. He remembered that, if he were to divide his money into equal amounts and give a little to each person in the world, there would not be enough to give everyone even a fraction of a grain of food.

So he determined upon a test. 'I will give to those whom I meet who are themselves generous,' he thought.

Dressing himself as a beggar, he went to various countries where he was not known. He made friends with people and asked them for loans. He begged from door to door in some places. He took menial jobs and worked in them for a while. And all the time he was making notes of the people who were gener-

31

ous, the people who did not take advantage of his supposed poverty.

He spent twenty years in this quest. At the end of this time he returned to the place where his treasure was concealed, and repaid, a thousandfold, everyone who had been good to him. Those who had refused him he left to their inevitable end.

THE PHILOSOPHER

I am thankful that the very bigotry of some academics is of value to the cause of sanity, whether they realise it or not.

A certain illustrious philosopher evidently frustrated by my answers to his questions, once roared at me—in the presence of some sixty other people who had up to that moment respected him as an objective person:

'Who do you think you are? One of your books is longer than the New Testament!'

THINKING THAT ONE KNOWS

People who think that they know all are often insufferable—rather like those who imagine that they know nothing.

THE INTELLIGENT MAN

A child, full of promise, was so intelligent that his parents and his teachers encouraged him to take an equal interest in anything which caught his eye, whenever he showed that he was attracted to it.

Years later, having tried a hundred different arts, and all the customary roads to success, he was penniless and miserable, and decided to take a job.

He found himself in the office of a millionaire whom he soon saw was fairly stupid and capable of understanding only one idea at a time.

'You can have the job,' said the millionaire.

'Thank you,' said the brilliant man, 'but I would like to ask you just one question.'

'And what is that?'

'I have read a great deal about you, how you understand everything you see, and how your extraordinary energy and wide interests have made you what you are. But I don't find you to be like that at all. Furthermore, I have tried since I was a child to be like that and—look at me.'

'Don't take it too hard, son,' said the tycoon; 'but millionaires like me pay people to write things like that. First, it flatters us; secondly, it ensures us a good supply of labour like yourself, people who haven't made the grade.'

33

HOOLIGANISM

A dog who happened to be in a specially virtuous mood once saw a cat chasing a mouse.

'Can nobody,' asked the dog of a companion, 'do anything to stop this kind of hooliganism?'

BEING

There is:
What one wants to know and wants to be.
And also:
What one *can* know and *can* be.
Deny these limitations and people will give you anything you want.

Affirm them and you have exercised true selfishness: telling the truth.

TALKING

I want you to take care of yourself, because next time I see you I want to talk *to* you, not *about* you.

And when I no longer have to talk to you, I want to be able to talk about you, for the edification of others.

ANTICIPATED

A student was spending time in companionship with a sage.

'If anyone were to say: "Stand on your head and you will attain eternal felicity," some people would do it,' said the student; 'people thirst for any directions, however inept.'

'My child,' answered the Sage, 'that is precisely what most of them have been doing these past ten thousand years.'

SOLVING PROBLEMS

No problem can really be solved merely by assuming that it can be solved and that its solution lies in hard work—any more than that its solution lies in inaction. Yet so much the reverse do the facts appear, that rabble-rousers and pretended mystics use the problem-solving argument to keep people busy. Solutions come through knowledge: so much so that where there is real knowledge, there is no real problem.

VIRTUE

If your own vice happens to be the search for virtue, recognise that it is so.

THE CHEESE

Once upon a time there was a cheese. A number of cheese-mites took up residence in it. As time passed, they bored more and more holes in the cheese, and, of course, they multiplied.

Then, one day, there were so many holes in the cheese that it collapsed into a powder, leaving the mites scrambling in the ruins of their home.

'What traitor is responsible for this?' screamed the mites.

They formed parties, each opposed to the other, whose objectives were to restore the former ideal situation.

Some mites, it is true, found another cheese. But as for the majority—they are fairly rapidly consuming the remaining cheese-powder.

BELIEF AND THE IMPOSSIBLE

There is a saying: 'I believe it because it is impossible.'*

But if you make any study of people in a state of what they are pleased to call 'belief', you will find that you can usually best describe them by saying:

'I believe because I am impossible'; or even: 'My belief has made me impossible.'

* *Credo quia impossible.*

WHY HE WAS CHOSEN

The disciple of a Dervish master whose name resounded from one end of Islam to the other one day visited the Grand Sheikh of Korasan.

'I have been honoured by my acceptance as a pupil,' he said, 'singled out from among the hundreds who approach my master every day, and yet are sent away.'

'My dear brother,' said the Grand Sheikh, 'I will try to further your education by giving you a piece of essential information. You were chosen because of being in the greatest need of teaching, not because of qualities greater than those of the other applicants.'

NEW NAMES

People rename things and even other people; this makes them think that they are different from what they were before.

Let us take a neutral example.

Have you noticed how even at present the majority of buildings are made of mud, but people will not have it that they live in mud houses?

Every home is also an imitation of a cave, but we do not think much of cave-dwellers, so they are called houses.

THE DERVISHES FROM
THE OTHER WORLD

Three dervishes returned from the Other World.

People, understanding that they had become altered, and wanting to follow their path, asked what had helped them.

'Pease pudding,' said the first.

'The Book of Wisdom,' said the second.

'Following a certain man alone,' said the third.

Some people thought that they were mad. Some thought that they were deliberately speaking in riddles. Some thought that this or that Way was the one to follow.

In reality, however, each had benefited from his own capacity and needs, in accordance with certain patterns which are only known to the men of greatest wisdom.

CLEVER AND PROFOUND

Statements which are merely clever and which have no development-potential, are often imagined to be profound, because they look or sound attractive. And profound remarks which have indeed got development-potential are as often deemed to be no more than clever.

THE REASON

The cat said:
'What funny faces mice have! That's why I have to destroy them.'

EPOCH-MAKING

People who feel it necessary to describe their activity as epoch-making are more often than not deluded. They try to make epochs because in this way their own importance will be created or increased in the minds of others.

What really counts is effect: not size nor noise, nor personalities, not even a sense of the colossal.

PERMANENCE

Someone quoted the proverb: 'Nothing violent is permanent.'

What a nice hope. I am sure that everyone would agree with it.

It seems a pity that the originator of this saying did not admit his hearers further into his wisdom, by giving an example of something which *is* permanent.

THE TOADS IN THE CASTLE

Once, in a reverie, I saw a community of wholly admirable toads. They had taken over, and made their home in a castle, obviously, to me, originally built by men.

I spoke their language, in my dream, and asked them to explain to me, as a matter of information, the origins and uses of the various parts of their castle.

They were kindly and hospitable toads, and they gave me full details of their lives and thoughts, and the way in which the building was used.

Every single aspect of the castle and its surroundings, including the moat and the marshes and reed-beds in which it was set, had a thoroughly plausible use and a toad-origin in theory, indicative of toad-thought and toad-design—conclusive to the toad-mind.

I said: 'Brothers, forgive my seeming discourtesy. But this place was formed, designed, erected, by other beings. It was intended for quite different purposes than you have mentioned.'

Some did not hear at all. The whole idea was so strange that it did not even register with them. Some said, shortly: 'You are a liar, or a cheat.'

Others, trying to help me, said to one another: 'Poor fellow, he is raving mad.'

That of course quite disposed of me.

THE MAN AND THE TIGER

A man being followed by a hungry tiger, turned in desperation to face it, and cried: 'Why don't you leave me alone?'
The tiger answered:
'Why don't *you* stop being so appetising?'

THINKING AND KNOWING

People think that they think things, and they also think that they know things.
They could usefully give some attention to the question of whether they know what they think and know what they think they know.

TEACHERS AND STUDENTS

People often say: 'I must find a teacher who knows all.'
Some, at least, of such teachers have started by learning wisdom from the ignorant, as some learn conduct from the ill-mannered.
Many aspirants could do worse than start at that very point.
When you have been your own teacher for a time, you may be ready to find someone else who can teach you.

THE DRIVER, HORSE AND CART

One day a driver thought: 'I'll let the horse and cart go where they like, maybe I am trying too hard to be the man in control.'

All went well for a time, since the horse took the cart on its accustomed route. But when the driver willed it to go another way, nothing happened.

'I need more will-power and less discipline,' said the man to himself.

One day the horse thought: 'Why should I obey?' And he started to pull the cart as and when and where he wanted to do so. The man sold him to someone who kept him on a very short leash indeed.

Yet another time the cart thought: 'I will assert my independence. At times my wheels will go, at others I will make them stick. Sometimes I will creak, sometimes not. And I will loosen and contract my nails as and when I feel like it.'

The cart, pronounced unreliable, was chopped up for firewood.

WHO CARES?

It is not only a matter of not caring who knows—it is also a matter of knowing who cares.

THREE WISHES

A man, after many years of study and effort, found out how to gain power over spirits. He conjured a jinn.

The jinn gave him three wishes.

He immediately wished for money.

Spending all his money on high living, he became an alcoholic.

His second wish went on making him well again.

Now he felt so undecided as to what to do, he used up the third wish to restore himself to his original state, and to forget his experiences.

HIGHER PERCEPTIONS

People imagine that higher perceptions might be attained by developing a certain inner sense.

But when a person has been working too much on the development of a certain inner sense, it is necessary to teach him by another method.

This method with the concept that the sense can be activated through the *exclusion* of factors which inhibit its operation.

Feed and exercise a lion in a cage: you may get a fine, robust lion. In order to fulfil his destiny, we may have to turn our attention from him to—the cage.

THE DONKEY AND THE CACTUS

A donkey was chewing some cactus.

A dog came along and said: 'What are you eating?'

'The most delicious of food,' said the donkey.

The dog took a bite at it. 'You treacherous wretch,' he cried, 'you have deliberately misled me, and now my mouth is full of spines. The taste of this abominable vegetable is nothing like the juicy meat which I was thinking about.'

POSITIVE AND NEGATIVE

The way in which a statement is phrased is not what makes it positive or negative. It is positive or negative in accordance with its significance, not its appearance.

A 'no' which is constructive is far better than a 'yes' which is not.

Because 'no' is something which people don't like because of having heard it often in their childhood, they tend to behave as if it were something bad: that is to say, unpleasing to them. It is only a step (though a mistaken step) from here to be able to call it 'negative' and therefore not constructive.

IN THE LAND OF FOOLS

Once upon a time there were three wise men. They belonged to a place known as Fuzulistan: the Land of Fools. But this, of course, was only what its uncharitable neighbours called it. The inhabitants called it The Country of Civilisation.

These three wise men decided that they would go on a journey, because, as everyone knows, travel broadens the mind: and even the most learned can profit by experience.

Quite soon after crossing the border they came across an unusual object. It was a minaret, towering into the sky.

'Ha, ha,' said the First Wise Man, 'Here is an item worthy of our observation. I will set you a test. How did this object come to be here, and what was the manner of its being produced?'

The Second Wise Man said: 'It is evidently a dead plant or tree. It grew from a seed, or even a certain kind of egg.'

The Third Wise Man disagreed: 'Not at all. This obviously was built. It must have been constructed lengthwise on the ground, and then hoisted to its present position.'

'You are both wrong,' said the First Wise Man, 'for it is evident that it was built by a race of giants. They were tall enough to lean down and place this thing here in its present position.'

It was concluded, after due consultation,

that suitable care should be taken by the expedition to preserve itself from the giants, who might, after all, be dangerous.

CONFESSION

'Confession is good for the soul,' an admirable sentiment.

It is valuable because it illustrates clearly something that its practitioners will ordinarily go to any lengths to conceal: that here they are not talking about a soul at all.

They mean: 'I have no conception of a soul, and therefore attribute the pleasure which confession induces in me not to its real source (the discharge of surplus emotional energy) but to something sublime.'

This is a fine example of the real information which we can collect from the hidden language of man.

Any number of comforting arguments could, of course, be found to deny or explain away this fact. There is no harm in listening to the arguments, so long as you are prepared to give an equal amount of attention to the observation of other people, to determine whether fact or argument is the more reliable.

THE SPIDER

A child, dismembering a spider, found that he was left with a number of parts. There were legs, a body and fur.

Being a logical child, he concluded that the legs were from a camel, because camels have legs, the body from an elephant, and the fur from a mouse.

Now an adult would never reason like that, would he?

DEFENSIVENESS

When people are told things which they do not want to hear, they produce or borrow certain standard arguments to enable them to exclude the new information from their relatively closed minds.

You can usefully offset this tendency by remembering that most unfamiliar information is likely to be met by this response.

Remember, too, that the things which you already know are mostly facts which would seem to be impossible, unlikely or even symptoms of paranoia to a man or woman at a lower level of culture than yourself.

It is this kind of understanding, not emotional reaction, which will enable you and others to face the truth, and to learn more.

THE SCHOLAR AND
THE PHILOSOPHER

A scholar went one day to see a practical philosopher, to determine the origins of his system.

As soon as the question was asked, the master handed the academic a delicious peach. When it had been eaten, the master asked whether he would like another. The scholar ate the second peach.

Then the philosopher said:

'Are you interested in where this peach was grown?'

'No,' said the scholar.

'That is your answer about my system,' said the master.

SUGGESTION AND ATTENTION

The effect of a suggestion tends to be in proportion to the prestige of the source of the suggestion.

Prestige is itself 'accumulated attention'. Accumulated and frozen attention.

Attention-fixing does not require the presence of the object. It may even occur, develop and become fixed through the absence of the object.

DRAGON

'It is a dragon, destroyer of all,' cried the ants.

Then a cat pounced and caught—a lizard.

UNDERSTANDING

One cannot guarantee human understanding, but one can help to develop it.

You can, however, enable others to understand only very little further than you yourself understand a thing.

This is why the human heritage of study materials is so under-used; the instructors are passing on only what they can—not what there is.

Understanding one level of materials is only a stage in passing to other levels. To compromise with one's ignorance by assuming that there is no higher level is a serious weakness. It holds back others, causes one to confuse the vehicle with the content, and is a disguised operation of self-esteem.

To believe that higher understanding is something which is not available to ordinary men is a mixture of the pessimist-culture's bequest and, paradoxically, self-esteem again: manifested in 'If I don't understand it, there is nothing to understand'; and, 'If I don't like it, it is of no use.'

TIME

Two microbes said:
'We may not seem to be much, but just you wait a little.'

MELONS AND MOUNTAINTOPS

If someone says to you:
'Do melons often grow on mountaintops?' do you imagine that this is bound to be an attempt to add to the questioner's stock of information? And that he is interested in melons and the tops of mountains?

Those who do not take such remarks as intended literally, interestingly enough, hardly ever go beyond the assumption that they are anything else than possibly meaningless or rhetorical.

The valuable thing about this illustration is that it shows how people can apply just three possible interpretations: literal, meaningless, rhetorical.

They certainly have the capacity to examine statements from other angles. But, since they have not been taught how to do so, they are not able, because too lazy, to adopt any other viewpoint, even experimentally.

CAT AND DOG

A cat and a dog were fighting. A man asked them what they were doing.

They said: 'The winner will decide which of us is a rat.'

'You are both wrong,' said the man.

So they set upon him, and put him to flight.

CURSE AND BLESSING

In the Middle East one of the major blessings which is also a curse can be found in the commentaries of the teachings of spiritual masters.

They are blessings for those who received them at the right time, and curses for those who ever since have struggled with them after they became anachronistic.

Few people would eat a piece of meat after it has rotted, or a vegetable when it has become a fossil. But almost none has yet learned about the equivalent problem in literature and traditionalism.

Let something become known as valuable, or sublime, and people's greed will do the rest. Even if the fossil breaks their teeth and the putrid meat poisons them, they will stick to outdated commentaries.

DOGS AND JACKALS

A man out hunting sent his yellow hound after something lurking behind a tree. The dog chased out a jackal and headed him into a position where the hunter could shoot him.

The dying jackal said to the hound standing over him: 'Have you never heard the Persian proverb, "The yellow dog is brother to the jackal"?'

'I have, indeed,' said the dog, 'but you are rather out of date. "Brotherhood" to the more civilised is connected with training and identity of interest.'

MAN AND HERO

Man really is a hero. Everywhere you will find him struggling for freedom and opposing its curtailment.

Yet very often he is obviously struggling for his own enslavement at the same time and with equal force.

To be obsessed by the idea of freedom, for instance, is itself a form of slavery. Such people are in the chains of the hope of freedom, and are therefore able to do little else than struggle with them.

WHAT I AM ...

A man sat in his room, thinking to himself. He said aloud:

'I am what I can make myself—what a challenge! What vistas, what opportunities!'

A piece of crumpled paper lying in the corner heard him. It said to itself:

'How excellent to know that my own sentiments are shared by others. This is indeed an inspirational situation.'

TABOOS, TOTEMISM, IMAGE-BUILDING

It has been fashionable for some time now for investigators to delight in observing and reporting on the local manifestation of these things.

It is useful to offset the parochial nature of most of such studies by remembering that these peculiarities are conspiracies to which the entire human race is party.

Observation indicates that taboos, totemism and image-building are tendencies strongly evidenced in the theories, action and exegetics of those who believe that they are only describing them.

DEMONSTRATION

It is narrated that Mulla Nasrudin was once trying to walk along the top of a very high wall which was only about three inches wide.

The crowd had gathered as he climbed to the top. When he fell down and twisted his ankle, people rushed up to him to find out what he had been doing.

'I have been demonstrating,' said Nasrudin, 'that you cannot walk along a high wall which is exceedingly narrow without falling and twisting something.'

FUNCTION OF RELIGIOUS SYMBOLS

When you see a traditional religious symbol today, you are generally looking at a piece of technical apparatus (or a representation of one), whose use has been forgotten —above all by the descendants of its own original designers. This is generally due to the growth of the superstition that a thing of beauty or associative significance has to evoke sentimentality, and that function is less sublime than emotion. The reverse, in fact, is the case.

A MOTTO OF
THE HUMAN RACE

Let me do what I like, and give me approval as well.

UNRELIABLE FRIENDS

You need not wonder whether you should have an unreliable person as a friend. An unreliable person is nobody's friend.

GENIUS

Note these remarks on genius, often quoted, but not investigated:

'Genius (which means transcendent capacity of taking trouble)'* And:

'Genius is one per cent inspiration and ninety-nine per cent perspiration.'†

Ignored or suppressed in these dicta is a major characteristic of genius. Both leave out the question of *manner*.

With these prescriptions you will not get genius.

Genius in order to operate needs the knowledge of manner.

* Thomas Carlyle, d. 1881.
† Thomas Edison, d. 1931.

WHAT A HORSE

There is a certain kind of horse that beats all others for speed. It certainly gets you there. When, however, it skids to a halt, the rider is thrown over its head and usually cracks his skull.

THE ANSWER TO A FOOL

The proverb says that 'The answer to a fool is silence'.

Observation, however, indicates that almost any other answer will have the same effect in the long run.

DUTY

No duty is ignoble. What can be ignoble is the sight of people trying not to be ignoble.

BOTH SIDES

To 'see both sides' of a problem is the surest way to prevent its complete solution. Because there are always more than two sides.

COMMUNICATION

For a long time now people have been claiming that what is wrong with society is that there is a failure of communication.

Many of these have had nothing to communicate other than the assertion that they cannot communicate.

They have communicated this effectively enough.

POWER

People say, because the phrase attracts them:

'Power corrupts, absolute power corrupts absolutely.'*

This, however, neither eliminates nor makes comprehensible powerful people.

The would-be righteous man should be able to taste the power-endowed man's feelings.

Instead of being nauseated by the following, he should be able to perceive it:

'Power is delightful to those whom it delights: absolute power, to them, would seem absolutely delightful.'

* Acton, First Baron, d. 1902: original version, 'Power tends to corrupt, and absolute power corrupts absolutely . . . There is no worse heresy than that the office sanctifies the holder . . .'

GENEROSITY AND WISDOM

How are generosity and wisdom connected?
Here is one way:
A generous person may not have wisdom:
but, unlike others, he has the means to gain
it.

EXAGGERATION

Exaggeration is a standard peculiarity of
man. To deprecate is often a form of exaggeration which people do not notice, because
it appears to be its opposite.

WHEN ADVICE EXCEEDS ITS FUNCTION

Advice is priceless: when it becomes inter-
ference it is preposterous.

SAYING A THING

It is not important to have said a thing
first, or best—or even most interestingly.
What is important is to say it on the right
occasion.

OPINION

Opinion is usually something which people have when they lack comprehensive information.

MYTH AND MAN

Man is a myth-maker.

Myth, when manipulated by unregenerates, is an even more effective man-maker.

Man (as he imagines himself to be), in general, is a possibility, not a fact.

For most people, the sort of man whom they imagine to exist, or assume themselves to be, does not yet exist.

CREDULITY

Learn to be as analytical about things of which you are credulous as you are of those which you criticise.

PESSIMIST

An egocentric pessimist is a person who thinks that he hasn't changed, but that other people are behaving worse than before.

AFFRONTED MAN

A man who, quoting the 'time' from a clock which has run down, has this pointed out to him by someone else—that is an affronted man.

SHUT DOORS

People often say that a door to something is, or has been, shut.

Do they, however, go so far as to investigate whether it has been locked as well?

When you really face a problem and see it clearly, you realise that it is not the door and its shutting which are significant, but the presence and condition of a lock.

This is one reason for informing the pessimist-cultures which imagine that their heritage is optimism and constructive response to challenge, that they need vision.

A response based upon inadequate data is not a response.

BELIEF

If you believe everything, you are not a believer in anything at all.

THE WISE AND THE FOOLISH

Fools expect themselves to be honoured by the wise.

But if the wise do honour fools, it is for reasons unsuspected by the fools themselves.

A frequent and diverting sight is that of some fools seeking honour from other fools. It becomes even more amusing when they are denied it.

WORDS AND THOUGHT

Words are an aspect of the attempted communication of thought. They are not thought. When we see words described as 'thoughts', we should make sure that we know this distinction.

TALK

You know him not at all—so you can talk against him.

You know him slightly—and you can boast about it.

You know him well—now you can talk against him again.

HIGHER EXPERIENCE

People who have been profoundly affected by having had a 'higher inner experience' should ponder the statement:

'When God wants to destroy an ant, he gives it wings.'

THREE KINDS OF LITERATURE

Note these three kinds of literature:

The first is factual literature, whose intention is to provide information.

The second is ephemeral literature, whose main function is to entertain.

The third is specific literature, designed to help develop capacities in a certain readership.

Literature which entertains may contain teaching materials as well.

TRUTH

A thing, an idea, a statement, is true only when and where it holds true. Something is true in accordance with its context. No context means no truth in the sense in which human thought understands it.

STUDY AND METHOD

Study is a matter of having information and knowledge of how to study, what to study at any given time, and what not to study. It is also essential for any advance beyond ordinary educational levels to be effective, for one to know, or to be able to apply under guidance, the matter of with whom to study.

Random study is no study. Studying things because they seem to be in one's field, or because they just attract one, is not real study.

Good discipline is a part of study, and exists for carrying out study: because it is the undisciplined, not the disciplined, who over-studies, and who amasses information which he cannot really digest in all its levels. Discipline also enables a person to focus on and off study, and to refrain from it when it is not indicated for the improvement of his higher states.

Although we must not shrink from the overt meaning of materials studied, on the factual plane, we have to realise that there are qualitative dimensions in study whose operating depend upon a knowledge of them. Those who do not know this have to learn it. Next, they have to find someone or some institution which knows how to do it, and is willing and able to communicate it in a practical form.

STIMULI

When a person has a jaded palate, as we all know, he needs more and more piquant and probably more varied taste-stimuli to activate it.

In current cultures, the result of over-stimulation of the mental palate is today obvious.

The analogy of the palate, however, is not completely exact, because the human mind has capacities of 'taste' which in contemporary societies are not satisfied at all.

The lack of this stimulus is because it is not realised that, in this area, a stimulus need not be intense in order to operate.

The result of this ignorance is that people will not give a 'gentle' stimulus a chance to operate, and reach forward to whatever seems most likely to afford them instant or deep stimuli.

Such people have almost completely put themselves outside the range of the less-crude stimulus. It is only when they are prepared to entertain the possibility of its existence, and prepared, too, to test its working, that they can be communicated with.

We can make no progress with a demand like this: 'Give me chillie-powder, but let it taste like rosewater.'

TASTING

He who tastes, knows.
But he who only thinks he tastes—will not leave anyone alone.

MEDITATION

Meditation without concentration and contemplation is not very different from water without wetness and coldness.

KNOWLEDGE AND POWER

Knowledge is power, they say.
But if only power were knowledge, that would be something worth thinking about.

TOO LATE TO LEARN?

If proverbs had been kept in proper repair, it would have been registered that:
'It is never too late to learn'—some things.
It is always too late to learn—other things.

DIFFICULTIES IN TEACHING

There have been communities and dedicated groups who have been given materials equivalent to a thousand years of teaching, and have hardly noticed it.

This happens for the same reason that people who are frenziedly greedy may not even remember what they have eaten—or whether they have eaten.

BORN YESTERDAY

Have you noticed how many people say: 'I wasn't born yesterday' and act as if they were only born today?

CHANGE EVERYTHING

If it were possible to do without food, there would be people who would urge its abolition. If one could live without eyes with any degree of comfort, there would be people to claim that they were the root of an evil. If time could be abolished, there would be people trying to get it done, on the grounds that we must have change, and not stick to old-fashioned errors.

SEEKING

You say that you have come to seek.

I have nothing to give you except the way to understand how to seek—but you think that you can already do that.

PREPARATION

In order to digest food, a man needs a stomach.

Who troubles himself to enquire, however, whether a would-be wise man is correspondingly well prepared?

SMOKE AND FIRE

The man who first said:

'There is no smoke without fire,' may have been describing the state of his contemporary technology, not enunciating a truth.

SHEEPSKIN

When you visit a sheep, do not wear a lambskin cap and claim to be a friend.

METAPHYSICS

I don't know how it is with other subjects, but I do know that many people who imagine that they can talk and think about metaphysics wouldn't know it if they found it in their soup.

QUESTIONS AND ANSWERS

One of the big differences between questions and answers is that, a question may be asked at almost any time and place, but its answer may come at a special time and place.

OUT OF THE TREES

People say:
'Only yesterday, so to speak, man came down from the trees. How, therefore, can he be anything of special consequence?'

And yet they seldom say:
'Look at that man over there. Only an hour ago, as it were, he was lying for eight hours inert in bed. How, therefore, can he be anything of special consequence?'

DESIRE

Desire without orientation is a game. What a pity that people should turn it into hypocrisy by pretending that it is something higher. When a game is being played, there is nothing higher possible to the players at that time.

THE DOOR SHUTS

When a door bangs, people look at it, attracted by the noise.

How few realise that it is at that time that they might instead be looking at another door opening or preparing to open one.

MIRACLES

What are called miracles, which people either believe in or do not, have a quite different function from what emotionalists imagine. They are useless if they only impress emotionally.

They are, in reality, either by-products and indications of some extra attainment, or exist to be recorded, inwardly, by a special organ of recognition.

DOING

See clearly how a man is doing a thing. You will then be in a position to see what he is *really* trying to do.

If you merely ask him, or enquire of a committed expert, you deserve all you get.

MAN

There is no inconsequential man. But what he has done to himself, and what has been done to him—that can make him inconsequential.

DEAFNESS

I have discovered a marvellous remedy for many forms of deafness: it is called 'praise'.

THE STAG

When the lion had eaten its fill, and the jackals had taken their share, the ants came along and finished up the meat from the bones of the haughty stag.

'I' AND 'ME'

Many people try to avoid using the word 'I', to show or practise humility. The consequence of this is to fixate them upon the concept of 'I'. They get the reverse of the effect originally intended.

What *is* important is to know which 'I' is involved in any act or statement. This comes only through the experience of the various 'I's in a person.

HIM WHO WAITS

They say, as you know, that all things come to him who waits.

We are not told, of course, what eventually happens to this well-endowed individual.

But, what a prospect! Not 'What he wants comes to him who waits'. Not 'What he needs' —but *all* things!

RAW MATERIAL

Listen to man: he thinks that he prizes himself above everything else. And yet he treats himself and his fellows as the cheapest raw material in the world.

SORE EYES

A 'Sight for sore eyes' is an interesting phrase.

Since no actual sight has ever benefited a sore eye, I suppose we could take it to mean that the incident is void of usefulness.

HARD AND EASY WORK

Prescribing hard work for the soft, or easy work for the hardy, is generally nonsense. What is always needed in any aim is right effort, right time, right people, right materials.

CONTRADICTIONS

Remember that things which appear to you to be mutually contradictory are, in real philosophy, only such because of the viewpoint of the time of looking at them.

Just as a child or an idiot cannot see how you can blow hot and cold—hot to warm your hands and cold to cool your soup—so can the underdeveloped human brain only think in comparably primitive patterns.

EVOLUTION

A man is deficient in understanding until he perceives that there is a whole cycle of evolution possible within himself: repeating endlessly, offering opportunities for personal development.

CHALK AND CHEESE

Chalk and cheese have far more characteristics in common than we would be led to believe by whoever framed the phrase purporting to illustrate differences by means of these two substances.

COMPREHENSIVE MATERIALS

If you are given something to study, regard well the conditions which attach to the study. That is to say, study it when and where prescribed. The materials and manner of study may very well violate the habits of study which you have formed in the past.

If you propose to study something comprehensive in an ignorantly selective manner, you might as well not start at all.

ATTRACTION

We all know people who are attracted to individuals and ideas either because these resemble themselves, or because they are in some ways their opposites.

The reason for the original attraction very easily becomes a barrier. There may be something in the person or the idea which can benefit the attracted: but this factor cannot beneficially affect the attracted person when he is still deriving satisfactions from the minor pleasure of being or thinking like or unlike someone else.

You may eat a cherry because you like its flavour. It will never, however, be of nutritional value if you keep it in your mouth all the time.

Proper study of this contention is exceedingly important.

BOTH ENDS

We are adjured not to burn the candle at both ends.

But how many people have verified that the parallel may be void, since it is not physically possible?

FOOLS

They say that there is no fool like an old fool.

I have, however, observed several: they were, as it happens, young fools.

SUPERCESSION

Try to wear the shoes which you had when you were two, four or six years old. You have a similar problem if you try, say, to follow a book of prescriptions written in Syriac.

If there is no supercession, there is no fresh growth.

If we are not to operate in the mode of today, we shall, at best, reproduce effects designed for people of yesterday.

THE CANDLE

'This candle burns for a hundred hours,' said the merchant to the blind man.

'I don't know about the burning, but I do know about the usefulness to me,' said the blind man.

UNWORTHY FRIEND

He is generous with what you have; and is economical with anything of his own. These twin practices have told you that he is unworthy.

Yet he can still convince you otherwise: because people believe mere words readily, and are eager for attention. They welcome sham actions.

The word, therefore, is speaking louder than the action.

THE DIFFERENCE BETWEEN SAYING AND DOING

Quite a common observation is: 'It takes all sorts to make a world.'

This may well be true: but if it is—where are they all?

SELF-SATISFACTION

If self-satisfaction follows an achievement, it was no achievement at all compared to what it could have been.

Depression after supposed failure means that the attempt was wrongly structured: no real attempt took place—however much it may seem that there was one.

BEHIND THE MACHINE

Man is generally a few paces behind his own inventions.

There are still many people who are revered as figures of authority merely because they can do such things as machines can do more easily. A common example is the awe which people show when faced with someone who has only a good memory or associative capacity, often stuffed with irrelevant facts.

This recalls the refrain 'man is not a machine' frequently used by people whose work and actions tend more and more to convert men into machines.

It is no accident that those cultures which most strongly and often affirm the value and individuality of man are the ones which do most towards automatising him.

GOOD AND BAD

There is no philosophical teacher nor system which will tell you to do other than good. You will probably be advised to strive against what is bad.

This is the first lesson, of course. But one should want to go beyond.

The succeeding lessons are not taught by inflexible principle, nor by ordinary cultivation, nor by standardised exercises.

The succeeding lessons are all on what is good and what is bad, in the successive stages of a person's life; in the different epochs of a culture, in the various expressions of a teaching.

You can only learn this from the exponents of a contemporary school, rooted in the most ancient past, expressing this in institutions designed to be effective. These are not made for attraction-value nor for the robustness of the vehicle.

YOUR PROBLEM

I have heard all that you have had to say to me on your problems.

You ask me what to do about them.

It is my view that your real problem is that you are a member of the human race.

Face that one first.

BOOKS AND DONKEYS

Anyone can see that an ass laden with books remains a donkey. A human being laden with the undigested results of a tussle with thoughts and books, however, still passes for wise.

SPECIFICITY

The analysis of a situation is one thing, the prescription of the remedy, when indicated, is another.

Diagnostic capacity does not prove therapeutic ability.

In dealing with human conditions, the procedure almost always has to be specific, not generalised.

M.C.O.

M.C.O. stands for Mutual Comfort Operation. One cannot understand the complex advantages and otherwise of human relations without knowing the quantity and quality of mutual comfort inherent in any social contact.

HISTORY

Right time, right place, right people equals success.

Wrong time, wrong place, wrong people equals most of the real human story.

THE WISE AND IGNORANT

When the ignorant have become numerous or powerful enough, they have been referred to by a special name. This name is 'the Wise'.

'BETTER TRY SOMETHING THAN NOTHING AT ALL'

This appalling statement holds good only in the most restricted fields.

A little radioactivity may be worse than none at all.

Try to cross a desert thirty days' journey in extent with only ten days' water rations —and then see whether the assumption given above fits your case.

Proclaiming, however optimistically, that the way to death is a way to life does not alter the outcome if it is attempted with no further knowledge than that.

TO FIND A WAY OF LIFE

Primitively damaging supposition under-
lies most people's thinking about 'higher
knowledge'. As a result, they ask the wrong
questions about it.

They may assume that inner studies are a
way of life. They are, in fact, a *means* which
produces the right way of life for each individual.

If you apply psychological techniques to
your everyday life you may make progress.
But they must be those which belong to the
time. And, if they are not suitable, you will
probably have on balance lost a great deal.

Many people are better served by self-
development which itself aims at transforming their outer life. But this is not a 'higher'
study.

INTELLECTUAL EXERCISE

I was invited one day to the delightful
home of a celebrated savant. Also present
were a number of his and his wife's friends,
all accustomed to the intensive study of contemporary as well as traditional human
thought.

After dinner, when we gathered in the
drawing-room, the atmosphere having been
prepared by three hours of stimulating intellectual exercise, the great man cleared his

throat, pulled up his chair, and addressed me. I could see by the expectancy on every face that this was the major turn of the evening.

'I have read such-and-such a book of yours,' he said, 'and I need not conceal from you that I regard it as being not at all what it purports to be, deficient in material and argument, not justified in its title by its content.'

'I am indeed obliged that you should have taken so much trouble with my poor work,' I said.

'I would like very much to hear what you have to say for yourself,' said the academic.

I told him that it was customary in the assemblies of scholars, so far as I was informed about them, to have detailed arguments before being able to attempt to defend oneself, much less to try to refute them. Would he condescend to tell me in detail what he did not like in my work?

He would, and did, at considerable length. He showed great familiarity with my subject, cited book after book to give other people's points of view, and generally gave a display of virtuosity which certainly impressed the rest of the company.

All this took about an hour and a half, during which time I, together with the others present, remained silent.

When he had finished, I said to him:

'You have certainly covered that field in an astonishingly impressive manner. Your delineation of my materials and the arguments against them are an experience. I wish that I could do equal justice to my own arguments in defending them, but I think that I lack your academic expertise.'

I then asked him whether, if he were in my place, he could marshal as impressive an argument from my own part. When he said that he could, I simply asked him whether he could do us all the honour of hearing it.

The result was that in just under another hour, so carried away was he by his eloquence and the joy of exercising his intellect, he succeeded in demolishing point by point, his own case against my book.

But the really strange thing was that the rest of the guests, accustomed to worship at the temple of this undoubtedly impressive man, congratulated him on his remarkable mind; not one of them seeming to notice that he had done my job for me, and had refuted himself and all his cited authorities in the process.

I only hope that I am wrong in suspecting that he would have gained an equal amount of adulation had he been reciting (from memory, of course) the London Telephone Directory.

REACTIONS

Psychologists have noted, quite rightly, that when people are guilty about something, they may react strongly against it, thinking that their behaviour is rooted in other reasons. We all know, too, that an energetic reaction may have nothing to do with the subject apparently being reacted about. We should watch these things.

But there is another kind of reaction, too. People who are accustomed to being stimulated by coarse or tense impacts feel odd when approached by an often more valuable, but generally more sensitive impact. They tend to avoid contact with this, by the simple pretext of calling it 'banal', or 'uninteresting'.

A sense of anti-climax is to be watched. It may frequently be caused by the desirable disappointment of an undesirable expectation.

You cannot be certain to be able to pin down the expectation which was incorrect, or even the assumptions which make you react in this manner. But you can observe yourself reacting in this way. This is an indispensible prerequisite for training to become really sensitive to essential impressions. It is called 'watching'.

CATERPILLAR

If you could say to a caterpillar:

'You were an egg, and you will become a butterfly!'

He would reply:

'Foul beast!' or else, 'You are imagining things, or seek to unhinge me!' or, again: 'I want to be one now, this instant.'

Or he might say: 'Who are you to tell me such things?'

Or, yet again: 'Yes, show me, while I crawl up this tree.'

MANOEUVRING

Many individual problems relating to perplexity and mutual misunderstanding would be solved if people could only appreciate that they tend to try to manipulate one another far more often than is suspected.

I have carried out hundreds of experiments in which I and my associates have, instead of taking people's actions and words at face-value, assumed that people are trying to score a point, or to assuage anxiety, or to manipulate.

This is the kind of experiment which almost anyone can verify. By alternately seeming to agree, to yield, to fall in with someone's suggestions or to be unconvinced, you can quite easily see this hidden pattern at work.

There are two great values in such a study. First, it helps you to dissociate your emotions from what is in fact a 'ritual' situation; second, it shows you what many people are really doing when they are at work or play, despite their own overt beliefs about their activities.

PEN-NAMES

From time to time I have had occasion to tell people that I write under names other than my own—pen-names.

Can you believe that, in at least nine instances out of ten, after hearing this, the person has said: 'Indeed? And what are your pen-names?'

This is a good illustration of the almost complete automatism of much thinking. If people write under pseudonyms, it is surely because they do not want their real name to be known as attached to that writing. Why, then, would such a person be thought likely to tell anyone else what that pen-name was?

This is all the more remarkable because the people reacting in this way were almost always strangers, comparatively—people who would be supposed less likely than close friends to receive such confidences.

THE FIRST AND LAST BATTLES

'Not knowing when one is beaten' is more generally only a pretty conceit than a rule of life.

There is a man better than the one who does not know when he is beaten. This is the man who does not have to know—because he wins.

On the same theme, some people seek to make a virtue out of 'losing every battle but the last'. I would, however, recommend them to win the first in such a manner that it is also the last battle.

In higher studies it is the people who have lost preliminary battles who are our greatest problems: for they may still be in the field, but have never escaped unscathed, and are generally in need of rehabilitation rather than instruction.

WHAT GOES ON INSIDE

When people say: 'I dislike your opinions, but I believe that you should have the chance of expressing them,' always beware.

Decades of observation, dealing with actual cases, has shown me that such people are, much more often than not, really saying:

'I am going to say that this person has the rights I have stated. I might one day get around to trying to live up to this sentiment.

But, meanwhile, I will use other means to combat his opinions: starting with making myself immune from them.'

Make a sustained study of reputedly fair-minded people before you accept their objectivity. Study their actions, and what they say to others, as well as what they would like to think they say to everyone.

PERCEPTION AND OBJECTIVE TRUTH

Suppose almost no human being could tell hot from cold.

People would then not be able to make use of heat or cold. They would be at its mercy.

They would find that water sometimes scalded them, sometimes was nice and drinkable. Why this should be and how they could avoid dangerous water and select good water might become a ceaseless search. While they were searching, the behaviour of water—and a good many other things—would make no sense: would seem to be motivated by some capricious Fate.

They would become superstitious about it. They would be attracted to anyone who could tell them something about it, or who seemed able to do so.

The fact would be, however, that they lacked an organ of perception, nerves which could signal to them when there was heat and when cold.

They would be likely to be in such a permanent state that they would actually conflict with anyone who told them this, though; because it would seem so trite. It would also seem patronising. And, alternating with their credulity towards 'teachers' of the heat-cold problem would be a demand to be 'shown' evidences indicating what was going on.

Someone might say, as we do, that the first necessity is to develop the perceptive organ, and that any argument which was left could come later. But the vicious circle would still be there: 'Tell me now, demonstrate it now.'

Again, since the organ of touch involved in distinguishing heat from cold is specific and cannot easily be described even to someone who has other senses, a lot of time and effort is wasted. People think that they can be told what 'touch' is like.

When it comes down to it, they can only experience it. Speech merely provides the aid to training 'touch'.

THE EXECRATED SHEIKH

In the country of Ardh there lived a cleric of exemplary habits and impeccable conduct. Over a period of many years he became respected by the people of his city and a favourite of their ruler. He won, by acclaim, the title of the Admired Sheikh.

From time to time he used to say to everyone, including his wife and sons:

'My example is useless to you, because admiration not followed by emulation is hypocrisy of the worst kind. Rather do the opposite of what I do, from sheer self-interest, than feel happy because there is someone in existence who is good, while you are bad.'

In the last quarter of his life he ceased to be a moralist and became a Sufi.

Inexplicably, the Sheikh's outward behaviour took a strange turn. Money entrusted to him by the king disappeared, rumours circulated about his morals during his absences from home, he refused his children the gifts which they had become accustomed to extracting easily from him. Instead of 'Admirable', people now called him 'Execrated'.

When he died his only remaining loyal disciple opened a letter which the Execrated Sheikh had given him long before, to be kept until his death.

The letter said:

'Dear friend, know the explanation of my conduct. Those who have imitated my bad example would never in any case have followed a good one. All I did was to exteriorise their delinquencies in order that they might one day find someone to cure them. The gold which everyone thinks I stole from the king is to be found in such-and-such a place, unspent. Return it to him. In taking it, I taught the king forebearance, bringing his capacity for restraint to the surface where it could be perfected. My wife had learnt patience and generosity through the test applied by my supposed misdemeanours, whose rumours I myself spread from the start. My sons can now support themselves in the world. By denying them what they desired I caused them to become adaptable and generous, for they do not want to be like me.

'But the greatest test is now upon you. Being faithful whether you understood me or not, you have perfected only loyalty. Now you have to understand that few things are always what they seem. Hitherto you have taken loyalty as the highest virtue. Now you must learn that it is the very lowest achievement in the ranks of the Elect.'

This is the origin of the founding of the school of the Execrated Sheikh, whose name is a byword of unreliability among many ordinary people, and equally the essence of perfection among those who know.

How people's folly protects them from good by itself appearing to be good! Even today there are many who say:

'The Execrated Sheikh had not the grace to confess his sins, even after his death. He went so far as to leave a letter which sought to justify his reprehensible actions.'

Such people are describing only themselves.

THE KING WITHOUT A TRADE

There was once a king who had forgotten the ancient advice of the sages that those who are born into comfort and ease have greater need for proper effort than anyone else. He was a just king, however, and a popular one.

Journeying to visit one of his distant possessions, a storm blew up and separated his ship from its escort. The tempest subsided after seven furious days, the ship sank, and the only survivors of the catastrophe were the king and his small daughter, who had somehow managed to climb upon a raft.

After many hours, the raft was washed upon the shore of a country which was completely unknown to the travellers. They were at first taken in by fishermen, who looked after them for a time, then said:

'We are only poor people, and cannot afford to keep you. Make your way inland, and perhaps you may find some means of earning a livelihood.'

Thanking the fisherfolk, and sad at heart that he was not able to enlist himself among them, the king started to wander through the land. He and the princess went from village to village, from town to town, seeking food and shelter. They were, of course, no better than beggars, and people treated them as such. Sometimes they had a few scraps of bread, sometimes dry straw in which to sleep.

Every time the king tried to improve his condition by asking for employment, people would say: 'What work can you do?' And he always found that he was completely unskilled in whatever task he was required to perform, and had to take to the road again.

In that entire country there were hardly any opportunities for manual work, since there were plenty of unskilled labourers. As they moved from place to place, the king realised more and more strongly that being a king without a country was a useless state. He reflected more and more often on the proverb in which the ancients have laid down:

'That only may be regarded as your property which will survive a shipwreck.'

After years of this miserable and futureless existence, the pair found themselves, for the first time, at a farm where the owner was looking for someone to tend his sheep.

He saw the king and the princess and said: 'Are you penniless?'

They said that they were.

'Do you know how to herd sheep?' asked the farmer.

'No,' said the king.

'At least you are honest,' said the farmer, 'and so I will give you a chance to earn a living.'

He sent them out with some sheep, and they soon learned that all they had to do was to protect them against wolves and keep them from straying.

The king and the princess were given a cottage, and as the years passed the king regained some of his dignity, though not his happiness, and the princess blossomed into a young woman of fairylike beauty. As they only earned enough to keep themselves alive, the two were unable even to plan to return to their own country.

It so happened that one day the Sultan of that country was out hunting when he saw the maiden and fell in love with her. He sent his representative to ask her father whether he would give her in marriage to the Sultan.

'Ho, peasant,' said the courtier who had been sent to see him, 'the Sultan, my lord and master, asks for the hand of your daughter in marriage.'

'What is his skill, and what is his work, and how can he earn a living?' asked the former king.

'Dolt! You peasants are all alike,' shouted the grandee. 'Do you not understand that a king does not need to have to work, that his skill is in managing kingdoms, that you have been singled out for an honour such as is ordinarily beyond any possible expectation of commoners?'

'All I know,' said the shepherd-king, 'is that unless your master, Sultan or no Sultan, can earn his living, he is no husband for my daughter. And I know a thing or two about the value of skills.'

The courtier went back to his royal master and told him what the stupid peasant had said, adding: 'We must not be hard on these people, Sire, for they know nothing of the occupations of kings . . .'

The Sultan, however, when he had recovered from his surprise, said:

'I am desperately in love with this shepherd's daughter, and I therefore am prepared to do whatever her father may direct in order to win her.'

So he left the empire in the hands of a regent, and apprenticed himself to a carpet-weaver. After a year or so, he had mastered the art of simple carpet making. Taking some of his own handiwork to the shepherd-king's hut, he presented it to him and said:

'I am the Sultan of this country, desirous of marrying your daughter, if she will have me. Having received your message that you require a future son-in-law to possess useful skills, I have studied weaving, and these are examples of my work.'

'How long did it take you to make this rug?' asked the shepherd-king.

'Three weeks,' said the Sultan.

'And when sold, how long could you live on its profit?' asked the shepherd-king.

'Three months,' answered the Sultan.

'You may marry my daughter, if she will accept you,' said the father.

The Sultan was overjoyed, and his happiness was complete when the princess agreed to marry him. 'Your father, though he may be only a peasant, is a wise and shrewd man,' he told her.

'A peasant may be as clever as a sultan,' said the princess, 'but a king, if he has had the necessary experiences, may be as wise as the shrewdest peasant.'

The Sultan and the princess were duly married, and the king, borrowing some money from his new son-in-law, was able to return to his own country, where he became known for evermore as the benign and sagacious monarch who never tired of encouraging each and every one of his subjects to learn a useful trade.

THE WISE MAN AND THE CRITICS

A certain wise man accepted an invitation to visit a town whose citizens professed themselves interested in his teaching.

He went there, accompanied by a small group of his disciples.

The sage gave a short address.

Some of the people said: 'We do not want a teacher, we want to know how we can find our own way.'

The sage told a fable.

Some of the people said: 'We do not want to hear old stories, we want guidance.'

The teacher spoke again, on some subject.

Some of the people said: 'This is not what we expected to hear.'

The teacher made a few remarks.

Some of the people said: 'We do not understand how this speech accords with the authoritative books.'

As the band made their way from the town, one of the disciples said: 'I fear that little impression was made, for those people only wanted to behave in a fixed manner, corresponding with the ideas already in their minds.'

The teacher said: 'Think well whether the purpose of this expedition was to instruct those who do not want to learn, or to demonstrate their abundance to those of you who may be able to learn.'

THE AIM

It is related that the object of Alexander the Great's Eastern expedition was to find the Water of Eternal Life.

They tell of the occasion when the great conqueror entered the cave in which the spring of life was gushing.

Just as he stooped to swallow a mouthful of that liquid, he heard a strange sound from the roof of the cavern.

Alexander looked up, to see a crow perched in the gloom.

The crow was saying:

'Stop, for God's sake, stop!'

The king asked him why he should not taste of that miraculous water. 'I have suffered much in order to be here today,' he said.

The crow answered:

'Great king, look at me! I, too, sought and found the Water of Life. As soon as I saw it I ran to the spring and drank my fill. Now, a thousand years later, without the sight of even half an eye, with my beak broken, my claws fallen off, not a feather left: all I ask is that which is impossible: I WANT TO DIE, and I CANNOT.'

Conscious that the aim must be formulated in accordance with knowledge and not just desire, Alexander the Great stood up and hastened away.

THE WANDERING BABA

Attended by a small band of disciples, Chara the Wandering Baba went on a journey visiting the many circles of dervishes which he had established in a number of countries.

In Samarkand, the Baba gave a lecture to his followers, and then spent several days separated from them, throwing tiny coins to all the children of the town, compelling them to dive into the river to retrieve them.

The disciples were not pleased, and the people of the town exclaimed:

'The sooner this ignorant and ridiculous dervish quits our neighbourhood the better.'

In Bokhara, the Baba gave out some teachings, then gathered the people together and told them jokes until the tears ran from their eyes. Some said: 'This is disgraceful for a man of faith, a teacher and Hakim.' Others thought: 'If this is religion, let us laugh our way to Paradise!' In short, everyone in that city became addicted to jokes and pranks.

In Badakhshan, the Baba initiated some followers, and then held classes in singing and dancing, until everyone in that remote province became involved in nothing else. Some people approved, others were profoundly dismayed.

When the party reached Kandahar, the Baba told everyone to stop writing and calligraphy, including illuminating manuscripts, until people bit their thumbs with horror and hoped that this disaster would soon pass over them.

Soon, however—such was the power of the Baga's example and energy—swimming became characteristic of Samarkand, Bokhara was the home of humour, and in Kandahar a school of painters and miniaturists grew up, because people had forgotten how to write.

Twenty years later Chara the Wanderer was dead. One of his disciples relates:

'I retraced the path which I had followed with my master, and it was thus that I realised what he had really been doing.

'When I was there, in Samarkand there was a terrible flood. Those grown men who had been children, taught swimming by the Baba's making them dive for pennies, took the rest of the inhabitants on their backs, and in this way saved them.

'When I arrived in Bokhara, a cruel tyrant had seized the city. He was strutting about, trying to impose his will upon the people. But they, accustomed to laughing at everything because of the Baba's jokes, laughed at him so much that he had a fit of apoplexy and fell down dead.

'In Badakhshan a group of evil men, anxious to extend their sway over the populace, had just brought drugs to the province when I arrived. They said: "Take these, and you will gain happiness and fulfilment."

'The people invariably answered them:

' "We do not need your drugs, for we are already completely intoxicated with the dances and revels which the Wandering Baba had brought us."

'In Kandahar, a usurper's edict demanded that all written records should be destroyed, so that all knowledge should seem to begin with his time. But the people—through the Baba's having stopped them writing—had already long since committed all their learning to another form of communication. The ancient lore was by now preserved in the designs on carpets, on ceramic tiles, in brasswork, embroidery, decoration of all kinds.

'Through the Wandering Baba, all these people and these things had been saved.'

UNNECESSARY

People who have organised their lives around the stability of relative ignorance regard all enterprises which do not fit in with their preconceptions as unnecessary.

They seldom pause to think, of course, that 'unnecessary' is the ideal term to preserve ignorance and especially timorousness: 'If the Good Lord had expected us to fly, He would have given us wings.'

These are the very same people who would have called scientific research unnecessary if they couldn't understand it within their own logic-system, but who would rush for antibiotics as soon as someone else had developed them.

It is 'unnecessary' for the monkey to start to believe that bananas could be cultivated, not just collected. Because he is a monkey.

It is 'unnecessary' for the savage to question whether fire is not occasionally sent down from heaven by a thundergod; or whether he could make it. Because he is a savage.

It is 'unnecessary' for a child to believe that we have to earn a living. Because he is still a child, even if he has to grow up.

It is 'unnecessary' for the adult to believe that he needs intellectual education if he is a manual labourer.

It is 'unnecessary' for the educated man to believe that he may need a different or higher form of education. Because he already defines his state as the best or highest.

But nobody can stop the process of learning, real questioning, even if only because our ancestors started on this course many thousands of years ago. They set us on this course, and we cannot escape from it.

LYING

Look at the phenomenon of lying in its relationship to fools.

Fools lie to explain or conceal their foolishness. It is not a remedy, but they use it.

Liars, again, are fools because a lie may be found out, and gambling fools are not different from the ordinary kind.

The liar fools himself that he will not be found out, and the fool fools himself that his lie will cover his folly.

It is not easy to avoid being a fool. It is possible to realise that one has been one. The remedy is not lying.

Again, it is possible to realise that one has lied, and to avoid it. Foolishness and lying being so much of a continuum, being truthful can help towards being less foolish.

It is for this reason, because it is constructively useful, that traditional teachings have stressed the need to tell the truth and be as truthful as possible. Truthfulness means being efficient, effective. Lying is an attempt to make inefficiency into its opposite.

This is why all forms of self-deception are 'lying'; and the person who foolishly cannot see the truth can approach it by practice in avoiding at least, for a start, some forms of lying.

Many durable 'moralistic' teachings are specific and effective exercises gone wrong.

DOUBT

Doubt others and they will doubt you. Do not doubt them, and they may still doubt you.

RIGHT AND FLATTERING

Not 'This man (or thing) is right', but: 'Is it flattering me?'

VIABILITY

You can keep going on much less attention than you crave.

MONSTROUS SUGGESTION

A psychologist I know noticed that a certain company was promoting its products with techniques which made its advertising nothing less than a campaign of indoctrination.

He observed the use of compelling rhythm and jingles, the tension and repetition in presentation, the breaking down of beliefs and the inculcation of new ones.

Instead of challenging the firm directly, he thought that he would seek additional information. So he wrote to the head office and suggested that they might well care to profit from the application of knowledge of indoctrination to include in their advertising.

Soon afterwards a letter arrived, signed by the managing director. He was revolted by the suggestion that anyone should try to manipulate the freedom of choice of members of the public. Not only was it, in his view, immoral, but there was a code to help prevent it.

How comforting to know that people in authority have set their faces firmly against such abuses.

LICHEN

A piece of lichen was growing on a rock.

In addition to the customary lichen thoughts, it often wondered why it could not spread so as to cover a part of the rock which was still bare.

'There is no lichen nutrient there,' said the wisest part of the lichen, 'and we must wait until it comes to us.'

As the years passed, the expectation of the mass of the lichen became stronger and stronger. Slowly, climatic changes caused the rock to split slightly. Certain chemicals were released and started to ooze outwards, covering a part of the bare surface of the stone.

For the devout lichens, this was the answer to their prayers, and they gratefully spread themselves over the delicious food.

Many years passed, and the chemicals began to become exhausted. This created changes in the character of the lichens, who attributed their difference in composition and being to profound social changes.

Theoreticians multiplied, each with his explanation. The lichen philosophers, academics and scientists divided themselves into groups. You can imagine what their various explanations were like. Each version was based upon the interpretation of observed phenomena. In fact, of course, the theories were generally attempts to concentrate and spread personal convictions.

Then another chain of events caused someone to spill upon the rock another lichen-nutrient, and the organisms were able to start growing again.

This stimulus itself energised the theoreticians. Their increased anxieties in the immediate past had sharpened their mental activity. It had enabled them to realise the immediate cause of their reprieve and comparative abundance.

But so far the lichens have not got to the point where they can fathom any perceptible intention behind the chain of 'causes' which brings them the means to live and to expand.

For this reason, they have given up thinking about it. They believe, nonetheless, that they *are* thinking about it. But that is only because they are at the level of culture which regards the following statements as 'thought':

'Everything is accident'

'Everything is of supernatural origin'

'Some things are accident, some supernatural'

'I do not know what to think'

'I can believe, and therefore I can believe that mere opinion is the same as knowledge'

'I have inferred some things, therefore they are true'

'I have observed some things, therefore I can observe others'

'What cannot be observed can be inferred, what cannot be inferred can be felt, what cannot be observed, inferred or felt cannot have any relevance to anything and is therefore nonsense.'

How fortunate that humanity is different from lichen.

THE LOG AND THE MUSHROOM

A rotten log was providing the nutrition for a growing mushroom.

As the fungus burst its way through the wood, it shouted:

'Down with this restrictive institution trying to inhibit my freedom!'

Other growths, which were spectators, were

much affected by the struggle. They said, in admiration:

'How beautiful is the irresistible heroism of fungi! What a lesson for our descendants. Let us never forget this day. That log thought that it was strong. Indeed, had it not been for the unconquerable spirit of the mushrooms, none would have dared to conceive, let alone carry through, such a glorious enterprise.'

Some toadstools, which had thrust their way with ease through leaf-mould, said:

'All this effort, this boasting, surely it is unnecessary?'

But they were soon silenced, in the rising clamour from the fungous chorus:

'Destroy, destroy, destroy tyranny, so that we may have harmony and peace.'

THE DEMON'S OATH

Once upon a time a certain demon overheard a pious man saying: 'Would that I could only be tempted, so that I could show that I am impervious to the wiles of demons.'

The demon immediately materialised before the man, and said:

'I am a demon, and I would like to take you on a pilgrimage to a holy shrine.'

'A demon on a pilgrimage?' said the pious man, 'this is surely something strange. But there can be no harm in going on a pilgrimage, no matter what one's companion is like.'

To the demon he said: 'I know good from bad, and it will be no use tempting me, you know.'

The demon said: 'Friend, although I am a demon, all I ask of you is that, during this pilgrimage, you will do nothing harmful to any creature.'

'Stranger and stranger,' thought the pious man. Aloud he said: 'I will swear that on my oath, demon, for it entirely accords with my own philosophy.'

'And,' said the demon, 'you will also have to swear that you will not kill, and that you will treat others with the utmost respect.'

'Agreed!' said the pious man, 'and if you are a demon you are the kind which I would most wish to meet, for it seems that you are already on the way to reformation. But if this is a trick, mark you, you will find that I am not susceptible to the wiles of the evil ones.'

'Fine!' said the demon, and they started on their way.

At first halt the demon said: 'What do you propose to eat?'

'Meat,' said the man.

'I will not permit that,' said the demon, 'because you will be encouraging harm to living things.'

'But it is not now living,' said the man.

'By eating it you are leaving a place for more meat to be demanded, and by causing meat to be demanded you are causing butchers to kill, and this is causing harm to living things,' said the demon.

So the pious man gave up meat.

At the next halt the demon said: 'Why are you moving that thorn-bush?'

The man said: 'So that I can sit down.'

'I will not allow it,' said the demon, 'for it will be causing harm to living things.'

'How can that be so?' asked the pious man.

'You have spent too much time in prayers for your own soul to notice that this bush is protecting the burrow of a rabbit, which will be left exposed to foxes if you take it away,' said the demon. So the bush remained where it was.

At the third halt the demon said:

'What are you going to do?'

'I am going to light a fire,' said the pious man.

'You may only do so if you can swear that it will not harm any living thing in the earth,' said the demon.

That night they slept without a fire.

The following day they came to a town. A man was coming down the street, and the pious man thought: 'I will show this demon, who seeks to make a mockery of me that I remember what I promised about doing people honour.'

So he went up to the newcomer and kissed his hand.

Immediately he was surrounded by infuriated local people who shouted:

'That man is a worshipper of the devil, and you show him honour!'

They seized the man and the demon and stoned them.

When they were eventually released they were within one day's march of their goal. The demon said to the pious man:

'Yonder lies the city of the shrine. I leave you here. Now enter it and do good deeds if you dare.'

DELIGHTS OF A VISIT
TO HELL

A man once thought:

'How I wish I could be master of the option, to be dead or alive, so that I might know what it was like to be dead!'

This idea so dominated his mind that he sought out a dervish and enrolled himself as his pupil. When, after many months, he judged the moment suitable, he said to his teacher:

'Reverend Sir, I have for years desired one thing: to be able to be alive or dead, as I wished. This is because I find it difficult to visualise what it would be like to be in that condition. Would you make it possible for me to achieve it?'

The dervish said:

'It would not help you at all.'

'I am sure that all experience is useful,' said the man. And he continued to plague the dervish, until he agreed.

'Very well,' said the dervish, 'adopt these special exercises, and you will be able to enter the domain of death and return at your own desire.'

The man performed his exercises until he had perfected them, and when he felt that he was ready, he threw himself into the condition which is generally considered to be death.

He found himself disembodied and waiting at the exit-door of life.

A subtle form in the shape of a man came up to him, and said: 'What is your desire?'

'As I am now dead,' said the man, 'I would like to see Heaven and Hell, so that I may be able to understand the advantages and disadvantages of each.'

'Certainly,' said the angel, 'and which would you like to visit first?'

'Heaven,' said the man.

The angel took him to a place where people were walking about surrounded by every luxury and dressed in beautiful garments, eating precious fruits. They were all undoubtedly beings of the greatest purity and honesty, but the visitor felt that there was not enough variety in their life for him.

He said to his guide: 'Please may I now see Hell?'

'By all means,' answered the angel, and took him to another place.

Here he saw people revelling and romping, laughing and crying, making and breaking friendships, building houses and destroying them, and living a remarkably similar life to the one which we all know on Earth.

But Hell seemed to have distinct advantages. It was more interesting than Heaven, and there were opportunities for personal gain evident to the visitor, which had not yet been observed by the inhabitants, and which far exceeded those open to people on Earth.

He said to his guide: 'As I am master of the option of living or dying, I think that I will now settle down in Hell. Can you arrange it for me?'

'Nothing easier,' said the angel, 'providing that you will change permanently from the status of a visitor to that of a resident.'

The man affirmed that he indeed wished to remain in Hell for all time.

Then the angel knocked on a door, and two massive demons of frightful aspect appeared. 'Take him away,' said the angel, 'for he has decided to join you.'

The demons seized the man, and crushing him in gigantic talons, began to bear him off towards a furnace.

'Stop!' cried the man, and he appealed to the angel:

'If this is Hell, what was that place which you showed me saying that it was Hell, when it was not?'

'That,' said the angel, 'is not the Hell for the permanent residents. It is the one which is shown to visitors.'

MONKS AND MODESTY

A monk, much respected in his community, said to me during a conversation in which he had become animated:

'*I* am among the most modest men in the entire world!'

He continued:

'I defy anyone to find, in a lifetime, more than five or six others as humble as me!'

What is, to me, awesome about this is not the man's own blindness to what by his own lights was a defect. It is rather the insensitivity of all those people who, when told this story to date, have sought to account for his behaviour by calling him, almost unanimously, 'an exception'.

People can live a lifetime without noticing that precisely this tendency may be (in one form or another) manifested and noted in our presence every day.

TWO GURUS

There were once two Gurus. They meditated and lectured, studied the lives and sayings of the ancient mystics who taught that man could control his outer life in order to attain release from the bondage of events and escape from the tyranny of the environment.

One of the Gurus knew the properties of secret herbs and had contemplated in the hermitages of the Himalayas. He had made pilgrimages and *darshan* visits to the abodes of Mahatmas great and small. He had attended the gatherings and rituals of the forests and the temples, and he was thoroughly versed in the mysteries of the sacred mantrams.

The other Guru, who lived at some distance from the first, had for many years instructed disciples. He had himself been a *chela* of several masters of high repute. He was familiar with the scriptures and the ancient classics inscribed on leaves, and he had measured his length along the ground in spiritual journeys, to countless monasteries. He had practised posture-training and mandala-gazing, had eaten the berries of the hermit and had worn the robe of the Sanyasi. He was regarded as a perfect Master by his followers, and by many who knew him and many who did not.

One day the Second Guru was visited by the First, who said to him:

'I have a young and recent disciple who wishes to attain *moksha*. I have sat with him and chanted over him, and I have also breathed on him and recited holy words, but he still seems very restless. I have exposed him to silence and to vocational exercises. We have meditated together and rung bells. The beads are never still in our fingers, and we have kissed holy relics. What would you advise me to do with him now?'

The Second Guru asked:

'Have you had him on a bed of nails?'

'No,' said the First Guru.

'Very well then, try that.'

A few days later the First Guru returned and said:

'It is with reluctance that I trouble you again, but I am in need of advice for my troublesome disciple.'

'Is he still restless, even after lying on a spiked bed?'

'I regret to say that he is.'

'Very well then,' said the Second Guru, 'I now advise a course of concentration upon secret inner sounds, hot and cold baths, and an application of holy oils and certain ancient breathing exercises.'

The First Guru went away, only to appear after a few more days, to report that all was not well with his *chela*:

'He seems to lack resolution, and the

course of holy efforts is not visibly taking effect.'

'We must resort to even more advanced methods,' said the Second Guru, 'and this is what you shall now do.'

He described a regime of special gyrations and callisthenics, the application of charms, a period of silence, special robes and several other secret and initiatory techniques and procedures.

Three days later the Second Guru was sitting with his customary serenity at the entrance to his Ashram when the First Guru again arrived.

'I suppose that you have come for further guidance for your disciple?' asked the Second Guru benignly.

'No,' said the First Guru, 'that is not now necessary, since the man is dead.'

'Dead? When did he die, and how?'

'He died suddenly, in front of me, this morning. He just went limp and collapsed. When I raised his head I saw that all life had departed from him.

'But did he say nothing before he died?'

'Hardly anything. Just before he fell to the ground he had started a sentence with the words, "When am I going to get some food?"'

DESERTS

People buy my books and sometimes take the trouble to write to me about them. Sometimes they send copies to be autographed. None has ever enclosed postage, so its costs me as much to post back their copy as I earn from it. Today I have had a request for an autograph, from someone who asks me to refund *his* postage. Do authors get the readers they deserve?

OVERWEIGHT

'This man is too heavy,' said the doctor who had been called in to see a patient in the Land of Fools, 'and his ailment will undoubtedly become worse unless something is done about it.'

He went home, leaving his knowledge and expected some action to be taken.

When he returned to see the patient, he was met by sorrowing relatives.

'Doctor,' they said, 'the man was sicker than we knew. Even after his weight had been reduced, he died.'

'Perhaps he did not get his weight down fast enough.'

'No, it couldn't have been that. We decided that the best way to take off weight was to cut his head off. We had that done in five minutes.'

BANAL

Banality is like boredom: bored people are boring people, people who think that things are banal are themselves banal.

Interesting people can find something interesting in all things.

MILK

A man who had come to visit me said of someone who had just left the house after a gathering:

'That man came in here looking exactly like someone who was trying to find a pint of milk!'

I asked him what made him so certain.

'Because,' he said, 'I used to be a milkman, and I should know that look.'

CRITICISING

Who is the wrong person to criticise?
You.

CRUDITY

Two people can illustrate crudity to you.

The first is the crude man, whom you see perceiving the diamond as a stone.

The other is the refined man, who makes clear to you the crudity of the first one.

SECRETS

A real secret is something which only one person knows.

GAMES

Denial and affirmation are games which people play.

There are people who deny that they are capable of denying, and who would insist that people do not insist.

UNDERSTANDING

People are always trying to understand.

There is only one way to do that.

It is to discover *why* you want to understand.

THINKING POINT

What makes you like me?

OVERHEARD AT A PARTY

'What does it matter whether we like one another or not? Surely it is the *deeper* things in life which really count?'

THE TALISMAN

Once upon a time a man picked up a talisman. One one side was undecipherable writing, on the other the inscription:

'Talisman for transforming stones and gold.'

He took the talisman to a place which was covered with stones, and said in the approved formula for such operations:

'Talisman, do your work!'

In the twinkling of an eye, the talisman had turned into a stone.

HOPE

It is not 'Have I got a chance?' It is more often: 'Have I seen my chance?'

ENEMIES

Enemies are often former or potential friends who have been denied—or think that they have been denied—something.

TEACHING

Teach honesty by all means—you do know what it is, don't you?

PERFECTION

Because there is a word for perfection, people will always imagine that they know it.

HATRED

If you want to strengthen an enemy and make him exult—hate him.

THE REASON

A man from the Land of Fools wanted to pull down the clouds.

'Why?' someone asked him.

'To squeeze out the rain.'

APHORISMS

Few things are more absurd than wise saws originally designed to inculcate or maintain the social needs of a society long past—when they are applied to today.

STIMULUS

A pungent thought is a corrective to deterioration of the thinking: like cold water helping slack muscles to work again. If you dislike the thought more than the sting of a shower which stimulates, and you do not feel its regenerating power—prepare for your mental obesity to possess you completely: it won't be long now.

BELIEF AND KNOWLEDGE

Knowledge is something which you can use. Belief is something which uses you.

SHADE

Have you noticed how many people who walk in the shade curse the sun?

HAND-CRAFTED

A 'spiritually-minded' lady more than once observed that I looked far too young to be a guru.

Some years of dealing with her kind has solved that problem.

Her objection now, I hear, is that I do not act like a guru.

For one with such a mind, she seems slow to draw the obvious inference.

People don't always get the gurus they deserve: they usually get the ones that they manufacture.

And why shouldn't they? Nobody else would have them.

CHILDHOOD

Once upon a time there were some discontented children. Since their thinking capacity was not very adult, they decided that they would become happier if they changed their clothes. Some of them started to wear one kind of dress, others dressed up all differently. Then some thought that their boredom and anxiety was due to obeying certain rules, so they changed them. Finding that this was no good, some of them started to invent one set of rules after another, and tried to observe them, each time convincing themselves that this particular set of rules would do the trick. There were all kinds of variations on this. They tried team-spirit, then they tried leaders. Then they decided that leaders were the trouble, so they decided all to be leaders, to exorcise this evil. That was not much more successful. Then they decided that certain inequalities were at the root of their difficulties, so they split into parties according to which set of inequalities was believed to be the most important. If they didn't like one set of rules, they inverted it and did the reverse, for they were practising sympathetic magic, like primitive people—though their name for it was rational analysis:

They are still at it, and seem likely to continue in this way for some time to come. At least, that is, until someone calls them in off the playground for tea.

OPINIONS

Do not ask people how they arrived at their opinions if you want the truth. By asking them you will only be entering into a game. They will only tell you what they think is true, or what they think you want to hear.

Study, rather, what they say and how they say it; what they do and what influences have played upon them in the past.

This is how you will find out, if it is necessary for you, how they have arrived at their opinions.

DEFYING EXPERIENCE

Every day man defies his everyday experiences.

He seeks simple answers for simple questions. There is no simple answer to a simple question when the question was defective: like, 'What makes that car travel?'

The answer, 'Petrol' is as true, untrue and incomplete and probably useless, as the answer, 'The driver, the sparking-plugs, the wheels, the transmission and so on.'

But the questions still come: 'What am I?' 'What are you doing?' 'What should a person do?' . . .

WAITING

There are a lot of people who cannot stand the tension of waiting.

These are the ones who have two alternatives: either to stand the tension of waiting or to be harmed by it.

GOLDEN RULE

'Do to others as you would have them do to you.'

Traditional philosophy has so deteriorated over the centuries that people have come to regard this trick-statement as a piece of advice.

It was originally intended to make people think. They were expected to react by asking why it should be a good policy, considering that most people want the wrong things for themselves.

SHORT CUTS

There are indeed short cuts to higher knowledge.

Those to whom the idea of a short cut appeals are the least likely to be able to use them.

This is because these tend to be the people in whom the factor of greed is so strong that it screens off the capacity to benefit from the short cut.

A straight line is not the shortest journey between two points if the distant point is so screened that you may see it but not reach it.

A man who arrives at the door of a house before anyone else may feel self-satisfied, not knowing that he has forgotten to bring the key.

WHAT THE CULTURE
TRANSMITS

It is the stupidity and shallowness of some of our forebears which punishes us, just as much as the endowment of the wiser ones offers us opportunities.

The rejection by the stupid of valuable materials in the past caused an impairment in traditional expressions and terminology. When this happens, the culture becomes unable to communicate experiences because it has no means of doing so: no patterns, and a mutilated language. Thought stabilises itself lopsidedly, like an organism which has compensated for the loss of one of its parts.

Colour-blind people cannot see colours.

TIME, PLACE, MANNER

Forget the fables of ritualised thought, so that you can remember:

The right thing said at the right time in the right way will almost never be the popular thing at the popular time in the conventionalised way.

Much knowledge is ignored, discarded or opposed because it is not apparently from an expected source, projected in a desired fashion, presented in a comfortable (or modishly uncomfortable) manner.

OUT OF CONTEXT

People often quote things out of their original setting or context.

'Context' in English means 'woven together'. Much wool is found woven together with cotton. But the co-existence of wool and cotton does not necessarily illuminate the meaning of either.

It is undesirable to quote anything out of its right setting or context.

It is equally undesirable, though very common, for things to be studied in an old context which was from the first unsuitable for them.

TOLERANCE

Tolerance and trying to understand others, until recently a luxury, has today become a necessity.

This is because: unless we can realise that we and others are generally behaving as we do because of inculcated biases over which we have no control while we imagine that they are our own opinions, we might do something which would bring about the destruction of all of us.

Then we will not have any time at all to learn whether tolerance is a good or a bad thing . . .

SHINS AND ARMS

Why does a dog sink its teeth into your shin and not into your arm?

Because, as an observer can see, the shin is within his reach, the arm is not.

This, however, would not prevent the dog from imagining that the shin is a more vital part than the arm.

No opinion is more tenaciously held than one in the mind of a person who has no real option to hold any other.

Yet opinions are generally substitutes for what opinions purport to be.

HAVE A CARE

If a Manx cat tells you that it is trying to preserve its long, beautiful tail, you don't have to believe it—especially if you have eyes.

CERTAINTY

What can you do with a person who says that he is absolutely uncertain about everything, and that he is absolutely certain about that?

OPPORTUNITY

People forget that when an opportunity is accepted, it is not what they may think it is. A man recognises and accepts an opportunity in accordance with the degree of man he is, and whether it is a corresponding opportunity.

ENDS

You are adrift while you still think that a means is an end.

SOCIETY

You say that this society will come to an end, because societies always have done so.

I wonder whether they have ended because they were not really societies at all.

FAME AND EFFORT

Effort makes some great men famous.

Even greater effort enables other great men to remain unknown.

PREJUDICE

People cannot handle prejudice because they try to deal with the symptom. Prejudice is the symptom, wrong assumptions are the cause.

'Prejudice is the daughter of assumption.'

DROP-OUT

We hear a lot about 'drop-outs': so much, in fact, that the people who talk about them have effectively attained their objective—to prevent us having the time to ask what it was that such people were ever in.

STRAWS AND CAMELS

Talking about straws and camels' backs is just one way of approaching things.

If you have enough camels, no backs need be broken.

OPTIMIST AND PESSIMIST

Sometimes a pessimist is only an optimist with extra information.

TALENT

Talent is the presence of ability and absence of understanding about the source and operation of knowledge.

UNRECORDED HISTORY

A philosopher of ancient times, after he had been dead for centuries, accidentally discovered that his teachings were being misrepresented by his living successors.

Because he was still a dedicated and sincere individual, he managed to transport himself back to ordinary life for a limited space of time.

When he eventually reached the Earth of the Humans, however, most of the people could not believe that it was him at all.

But when he had convinced some people that he had really returned, some said:

'Your being able to come back here is far more interesting than your ideas: don't you see that?'

So he made no progress with them, and had considerable difficulty in escaping their attentions.

The people who realised that he really was himself, said:

'Do you not understand that the most important thing is not what you said or did, but what *we* believe you said or did?'

'*You*, after all, are a transient here. *We* are continuous.'

DID YOU?

Did you ever hear of the man who heard of a certain buried treasure? It was in a country where a foreign language was spoken. It was to be given to someone who exactly answered his description.

A friendly and well-intentioned man offered to teach him the Chinese language before he set off.

He had spent so much time in learning the language that he thought he'd better invest in a horse, to get him to the hoard before he was too old to enjoy it.

When he got there, however, he found that Chinese was not the language spoken in that country. And when he did find the spot, and could communicate with the people about the treasure, they said:

'You can certainly have the treasure; but for one small point upon which you have unfortunately not informed yourself: the man who buried it specifically excluded from its future possession anyone who rides a horse.'

THE FIRST APE AND
THE BANANAS

There was once an ape who discovered, in conversation, that there were such things as bananas.

This information stimulated his innate affinity for bananas.

For years he dreamt of the day when he would eat one.

In the fullness of time a bunch of bananas came his way.

Eating them was a sublime experience, as marvellous as he had imagined that it would be.

But from that day on, he was unhappy. He decided that he would never again have the chance of such a stimulus, anticipation and fulfilment, as now lay behind him.

Because of this belief, the ape became impossible to live with. Eventually he lay down and died.

THE SECOND APE AND
THE BANANAS

There was an ape who wanted a banana more than he wanted anything else.

When he eventually got one, its taste fulfilled his highest expectations.

Next time he was offered one, however, it did not seem to taste at all good.

In fact, his original experience of banana-eating had been compounded of nine-tenths anticipation and one-tenth banana.

When he tasted the banana this time, therefore, he spat it out, saying:

'*That* is not what I call a banana. Someone is evidently trying to deceive me!'

He passed most of the rest of his life trying to find the right kind of banana.

Ultimately he decided that his first banana had been unique, so he gave up the search.

DEATH

A man once said:

'Death? That's something I'll believe in when I have some evidence for it.'

He went to a mountaintop to contemplate, and refused to see or to listen to any living creature, since his investigations into death were of the greatest importance to him.

That was thousands of years ago.

Since nobody has ever heard of him again, nobody knows whether he is still alive or not.

Even history has forgotten about him, which goes to show how ungrateful humanity is towards its heroic investigators.

EVOLUTION

In a certain forest the monkeys used to throw sticks to make fruit fall from the trees. But, just as they had at one time acquired this art, they were quite able to develop beyond this stage.

One morning a certain monkey saw that a spider had spun a web, and could get to his food by scurrying across it. '*That* is an advanced way of doing things,' said the primate to himself.

So he asked the spider how to do it. When there was no reply, he killed the insect with an impatient blow. Then he described the idea to his companions. They spent an enormously long time trying out various webs fashioned from creepers, of bark, even of saliva. Schools of thought and chattering institutes of study based on the feasibility of this technique grew up . . .

But then a whole afternoon had almost worn to an end, and the monkeys were hungry again. It would soon be dark.

One by one they wandered off in search of suitable sticks to throw up at the laden trees . . .

GRIT

'What you are pleased to call a mere piece of grit,' said the oyster, 'is in reality nothing nearly so simple.

'It is a socio-psychological problem of ever-shifting emphasis and real elevance to contemporary circumstances.

'To speak of it in terms of a "process" is to try to mock the entire intellectual and academic heritage of oysterdom.

'No oyster could have any patience with you.'

WORRIED

A mosquito was buzzing around the ear of a tiger.

The tiger, from time to time, shook his head or raised a paw towards his ear.

Another insect flying past watched for a moment. Then he said to the mosquito:

'You will never survive if you go near enough to taste any of the tiger's blood.'

'I do not intend to try,' said the mosquito, 'but I have made him worried, have I not?'

TRUTH

From time to time ponder whether you are unconsciously saying:

'Truth is what I happen to be thinking at this moment.'

COMMON KNOWLEDGE

The more you look at 'common knowledge,' the more you realise that it is more likely to be common than it is to be knowledge.

No real knowledge is common.

TWO RELIGIONS

I asked a venerable authority:
'What would you call these beliefs?
"Man was born to suffer; for he has to suffer, to be born again." '
He said:
'This is Christianity, without a doubt.'
Then I asked another equally hoary pundit the same question.
His answer was:
'That statement summarises the spiritual philosophy of Hinduism.'
Life *is* difficult, isn't it?

EXPECTATION

If, from time to time, you give up expectation, you will be able to perceive what it is you are getting.

GIVING AND TAKING

If you give what can be taken, you are not really giving.

Take what you are given, not what you want to be given.

Give what cannot be taken.

LIFE AND DISAPPOINTMENT

Seeing an old lady of evident serenity and knowledge sitting opposite me on a train, I leant forward and asked her:

'What wisdom can you pass on to me?'

She said:

'Young man, all I have got to say is that life has been a great disappointment to me!'

TANTALISING

People wonder why, as they put it, Eastern teachings tantalise. It is generally because once we can see that people have become tantalised, they are not yet ready for true understanding.

How can you be tantalised by something which is not in itself appetising, if you are not yourself greedy?

WHAT DID YOU LEARN?

Please, not again what you studied, how long you spent at it, how many books you wrote, what people thought of you—but: *what did you learn?*

RIGHTS

A man jealous of his own rights often manifests this covertly working for himself, by fighting for the rights of others.

The weakness of such a situation is that people have still not realised that rights based on any jealousy are not worth having.

PEOPLE AND IDEAS

The devil said to the scholar:

'Why do you make yourself master of an entire field of learning, so that people can be guided by you out of total ignorance into comparative knowledge?'

The scholar said:

'I like the idea, but not the person who suggested it.'

'That is good enough for me,' said the devil, 'for people easily forget the person, as soon as they can make use of an idea.'

FOR EXTRA-TERRESTIAL
BEINGS

When the human being says:
'It is not true . . .'
He may mean:
'I don't know about it, so I think it is un-
true.'
Or:
'I don't like it.'

DECISIONS

People who 'cannot make decisions' are
in that state because they have made a decision not to make decisions.

They are indecisive because they have been
too decisive in the first place.

The consequence of precipitate decisive-
ness must be inactivated, if the condition of
uncertainty is to be to overcome.

BIG AND SMALL

The only drawback about being too big for
small things is that it makes one too small
for big ones.

Too big for information is equal to too
small for knowledge.

Too big to learn means too small to understand.

When anyone says 'I am beyond *that*', you may be sure that *it* is beyond *him*. Not because it must be beyond him, but because if he were beyond it, he would not say it.

WETTER WATER

We all know people who want water to be wetter.

They need to realise that water is there to be of the wetness of water.

To agree with such people's first assumptions is hypocrisy or ignorance, To try to wetten water for them is stupidity.

TOURISM

A tourist is a person who goes to a place which was originally worth visiting. He is undoubtedly endowed with supernatural powers, because after sufficient exposure to the tourist, the inhabitants start to hate the place.

TOYS

People used to play with toys.
Now the toys play with them.

REMEMBERING AND FORGETTING

You have not forgotten to remember;
You have remembered to forget.
But people can forget to forget. That is
just as important as remembering to remember—and generally more practical.

ADVANCED

What is sometimes thought to be clever is,
significantly often, merely an advanced form
of foolishness.

SHRINKAGE

Water shrinks wool, urgency shrinks time.
Shrinkage may be an advantage or the
reverse, according to expectation.

AGAINST GOD

How curious that people should be more
interested in the charge that I am 'against
God', than in the question whether God is
against *me*.

THE EMPEROR'S NEW CLOTHES

It is not always a question of the Emperor having no clothes on. Sometimes it is, 'Is that an Emperor at all?'

DIGESTION

Instead of giving one a religious tract, people interested in that kind of thing ought to make sure first that the recipient has a *digestive* tract, to be able to absorb the real content of spiritual materials.

VERSATILE THOUGHT

While you use thoughts which attract or repulse you only for purposes of stimulation, you are only half alive. You are also co-operating in keeping yourself in good training to be conditioned by others.

WHAT DO YOU THINK I AM?

The stupidest man I ever met had a favourite saying.

It was:

'What do you think I am, stupid, or something?'

LAZINESS

The laziness of adolescence is a rehearsal for the incapacity of old age.

THE SEEKING OF THE MASTER

Musa Najib was asked why he charged a fee from those who came to his sessions; and why he often did not even address his audience.

He said: 'I charge for this object lesson: people believe that knowledge must be given freely, and consequently mistake everything which is free for knowledge. I do not always lecture because, among Sufis, "The Master finds the pupil." The pupil has to be physically present: but he may be absent in every other sense. When I discern that a pupil is "present" then I "find" him, for then his inner call is audible to me, even if it is silent to him.'

'Seek and you will be found.'